Fair Isle Sweaters Simplified

ANN BOURGEOIS
EUGENE BOURGEOIS

Martingale
& COMPANY

BOTHELL, WASHINGTON

P9-DXE-330

Fiber Studio Press is an imprint of Martingale & Company.

President . . . . Nancy J. Martin
CEO . . . . Daniel J. Martin
Publisher . . . . Jane Hamada
Editorial Director . . . . Mary V. Green
Technical Editor . . . . Jane Townswick
Copy Editor . . . . Karen Koll
Design and Production Manager . . . . Stan Green
Cover Designer . . . . Trina Stahl
Text Designer . . . . Stan Green
Illustrator . . . . Robin Strobel
Photographer . . . . Philip Walker
Photographer's Assistant . . . . Leanna Smith

Fair Isle Sweaters Simplified
© 2000 by Ann Bourgeois and Eugene Bourgeois

Martingale & Company
PO Box 118
Bothell, WA 98041-0118
www.patchwork.com

No part of this product may be reproduced in any form, unless otherwise stated, in which case reproduction is limited to the use of the purchaser. The written instructions, photographs, designs, projects, and patterns are intended for the personal, noncommercial use of the retail purchaser and are under federal copyright laws; they are not to be reproduced by any electronic, mechanical, or other means, including informational storage or retrieval systems, for commercial use. Permission is granted to photocopy patterns for the personal use of the retail purchaser.

The information in this book is presented in good faith, but no warranty is given nor results guaranteed. Since Martingale & Company has no control over choice of materials or procedures, the company assumes no responsibility for the use of this information.

Printed in China
05 04 03 02 01 00   8 7 6 5 4 3 2 1

Library of Congress Cataloging-in-Publication Data
Bourgeois, Ann
    Fair Isle sweaters simplified / Ann and Eugene Bourgeois.
        p. cm.
    "Philosopher's wool"—Cover.
    ISBN 1-56477-311-6
        1. Knitting—Scotland—Fair Isle—Patterns. 2. Sweaters—Scotland—Fair Isle. I. Bourgeois, Eugene II. Title.
    TT819.G7 B68 2000
    746.43'20432—dc21   00-026002

MISSION STATEMENT
We are dedicated to providing quality products and service by working
together to inspire creativity and to enrich the lives we touch.

This book is dedicated to knitters everywhere.

Lorraine
Remember

Don't (want)
Do (want)
Out
& Through

Ann & Eugene
2001 Puyallup

CONTENTS

INTRODUCTION

THE PHILOSOPHER'S ROAD TO SHEEP

Eugene Bourgeois

WHEN ANN AND I set out to build our farm, and subsequently our business and our lives, neither of us was qualified as a builder nor a farmer. My previous experience with design and construction consisted of making a table for my sister, who was always moving. I decided that it should be completely collapsible so she could pack it up easily. I also thought that since she was moving so much, it should perhaps be built like a sailboat, with a central post and four off-centered legs, all held together by a rope that looked like the rigging of a sail. It was a wonderful design whose only problem was that it collapsed any time it was used. When Ann and I announced to my parents that we were going to build a farm, my mother could only wonder how I was ever going to get a house to stand up.

At the time, Ann and I and our two children were living in a rented stone farmhouse on the outskirts of a southwestern Ontario town called Waterloo. The natural setting seemed both healthy and contemplative. There was a huge barn adjacent to the rented house. We had a garden that provided all our basic vegetable needs. It was a very rural environment, and we fancied that we were living the life of farmers. We adapted easily to the rhythms of the farming calendar, tilling, planting, and harvesting.

In the woods nearby, I found many different wild mushrooms. I learned to identify them and to cook with the safe ones. I thought there must be a market for them in the gourmet restaurants of Toronto.

Ann taught while I pursued an M.A. in Pythagorean mystical philosophy at the University of Waterloo.

We lived modestly and were able to save a large portion of Ann's teaching salary. We made plans for the farm we would build and made field trips to find a suitable piece of land. I believed a ten-acre farm could provide all the nourishment and shelter a family would need. I believed then, and still do today, that Pythagorean mysticism was all that was needed to build a farm. If you know that the square on the hypotenuse is equal to the sum of the squares of the other two sides, do you need anything else? Well, maybe.

It was 1974, the time of the first oil crisis, and inflation was rampant. People were escaping the cities, and many also seemed to think that ten acres was a perfect size of property to provide them the isolation they craved. They had cash from city real estate. We had our savings, which amounted to very little. We were having little luck finding a farm we could afford when my parents chanced upon a small parcel of land for sale near Inverhuron Provincial Park on the shores of Lake Huron.

It didn't look like much when we first set our eyes on it. Gordon Buchanan, who would become our neighbor, sat on his W4 tractor nearby, chewing tobacco and listening as the local real estate agent insisted that this was the property of our dreams. When all was said, Gordon, then in his mid-seventies, took me aside and told me to buy this land because it was a good piece of land. That decided me on the purchase. The wild strawberries in the rocky, scrubby second field decided the children on the land. The proximity to Lake Huron, such a large body of water, decided Ann. We were able to make the down payment and have enough money left to get a well

dug. We set out to finance the building of our home.

The banks were disinclined to get involved with our plans and refused to give us a mortgage. These were the days when a fully employed woman like Ann would be asked the question, "Where does your husband work?" The answer "philosophy student" was not satisfactory. Bankers seemed to intuit that there was a limited market for philosophy graduates, especially those of a Pythagorean mystical bent. We were at loggerheads. They claimed I had no experience or knowledge of farming and was a bad risk. I said it was my experience that many farmers were philosophers, and thus I was highly qualified.

We agreed to disagree. We decided to build as much as we could with whatever we might save that year and I enlisted the help of my uncle, who is a builder. He agreed to help me build our farmhouse and we planned to do it the next summer, in 1975. I designed the house while writing the draft of my thesis. The University of Waterloo is a great engineering school and I had many friends in engineering and systems design who lent a hand. Our house is a

traditional Ontario-style farmhouse, red brick with yellow brick trim around the doors, windows, and corners. My goal was to make it as energy efficient as possible, using passive solar designs to capture as much winter heat as possible without overheating us during the summer. I also wanted to build a house that blended into the background. When we later learned that our house was known locally as "the new old house," I knew we had succeeded.

I took a leave of absence from the university's summer term. My uncle arrived with his sixteen-year-old twin sons. We set up camp on our land with a tent and my parents' tent trailer. While I was off getting the lumber for the house, my uncle started the excavations. It was a perfect day and the night of the full moon. That month was hot and dry, except for one rainy day just after we poured the concrete for the foundation. By the next full moon the house was framed and my uncle said goodbye. We had the shell of our house and we walked about endlessly, looking at the views from what would be our rooms. I thought we were almost finished. There were, after all, only the interior walls, windows,

electrical and plumbing work, insulation, flooring, and plastering to do.

During what became the long, then increasingly longer period of interior construction, I often wandered through our property and the local park area. I began identifying mushrooms that grew locally and discovered that many of the edible local varieties were delicious. My dream of supplying the Toronto restaurant market with exotic mushrooms returned: I thought that we should grow exotic wild mushrooms in the root cellar under the veranda.

The problem with growing wild mushrooms was that no one was doing it. There are woodland and grassland species. The woodland species could be grown on sawdust and wood chips and there were plenty of small sawmills locally that would provide me with the substrate necessary. For the grassland species, we needed a source of compost. Literature on the subject suggested that domesticated sheep produce a lot of composting material each year. And so, with that particular product in mind, I enrolled in a sheep management course.

THE TUDOR AND THE BARN

WE SPENT THE next five years building. We bought a log cabin that I moved to our site before local authorities said we had to join it to the house we were building. I decided to learn to timber frame and to build a Tudor-style addition that would join the two buildings. I had some sense of timber framing, having torn down a timber-framed drive shed that we planned to reconstruct as our barn. But those timbers were rotted, and as I was removing the roof, the building collapsed under me. I rode the roof down and jumped off at the last moment, landing on the roof again as it bounced up from the fall. Unscathed, I decided to save the roof sections to use as a shelter for chickens and pigs.

As we were moving the log cabin, I had the good fortune to meet Jack Spitzig, an elderly gentleman who had retired from timber framing and had, during his time, built many of the local barns. He agreed to teach me to build, so I set about designing our barn. Ann continued to teach part-time. Our neighbor, Gordon, kept buying old farm machinery at auctions for me and taught me how to repair and rebuild them. He had a blacksmith shop and showed me how to make parts to replace those that were unavailable.

I was out one day looking at the site we intended to use for the barn, wondering how we would find the money to build it. We had saved about $2,000, and I knew this would be inadequate. As I was considering what to do, the idea struck me that this was the day I had to start our barn. This seemed totally absurd to me, and I tried my best to get rid of the notion, but the idea

just wouldn't go away. Feeling somewhat foolish (but well aware that the fool is a central icon of mystical philosophy), I began to lay out the building site with string, hoping that something sensible would occur in the meantime. Nothing did.

The next step was to excavate for the footings. I could call in heavy machinery and it would be done in a day. But then what would I do? I'd have even less money to buy the timber I needed. I decided instead to do the foundation by hand and spent the next month digging the trench that would become the forms for our footings and foundation walls. We got needed rain just after pouring the concrete. Jack Spitzig was anxious to help me start building, but I was still without the right wood for timber framing.

I decided to go for a drive. During the sheep management course I had taken, I heard about an Amish sawmill that had oak lumber. The barn would need wooden pegs, and oak was the best material for them. I had only a vague idea where this mill was and I set off hoping to find it. I made a wrong turn and was thinking about how to get back when I came upon the mill. What luck!

I looked about and noticed some heavy oak slabs, which would make great pins for the barn. The mill owner, John, said no one in his community timber-framed any more. He said he'd be glad to sell me whatever I needed. I asked, idly, how much it would cost for me to buy white oak timbers, including four that would be twenty feet long. He quoted an astonishing price of $500 per thousand board feet. Even spruce two-by-fours cost $635 per thousand board feet; could John really mean what he said? I'd been thinking I could only buy a few timbers to replace the ones that were seriously rotted or damaged. If this price was firm, I could afford an entire new set of oak timber.

The more we talked about the virtues of timber buildings compared to contemporary farm buildings, the more the price fell. The clincher came when John asked if I had a boring machine, which is the portable drill press that's used to make the pinholes. I said I did, that my neighbor had told me that if I was going to build a barn I'd need one of these and had sold me his for $10. John said that if my neighbor could sell me the machine for such a low price, he would sell me the timbers for $400 per thousand board feet, take it or leave it. I said that I'd love to take the price, but I had to check first with Jack, the timber framer, to see just how much I'd need and whether the white oak would be suitable material for my barn. As I was leaving, John asked me to wait for a minute. He went to his shop and returned with a handful of boring machine bits. Did I have any of these, he asked? I said that I didn't and he handed them to me, telling me that I would certainly need them if I were going to timber frame. I promised I'd be back the next week.

When I told Jack what I'd found, his mouth hung open. "White oak," he'd repeat to himself. He had always wanted to build a barn with white oak but never had because of its expense. This, he said, was a great price for it. During the 1940s, when he was forest manager for a major concern here, they sold all the white oak they harvested to the Massey Harris company for axles. The selling price then was for just more than $400 per thousand board feet. Was I sure he had given me the right price? I went to the local building supply store and asked them what white oak timber would cost. If they could get it, they stressed, it would be around $4,000 per thousand board feet. Had I heard the wrong number?

I went back to the sawmill and John was there to greet me. I told him what Jack had said and gave him a complete and extensive list of

materials I would need. John, who also owned a farm, said that they would cut the material as soon as his crop was finished, as all of the boys were out in the fields. That was fine with me because I still had lots to do, and we set about making the rafters. I checked again about the price. As I tallied the costs of the lumber, it came to just more than $1,000, a price that seemed to me unbelievably low. John assured

me that the price was right and he was well satisfied with it. As the days wore on we finished all the preliminary work and still the timbers hadn't arrived. I kept driving out to check and the story was always the same: the boys were out with the crop. September had begun and the boys were still out with the crop. John said that he just couldn't do the work because he was short by two men. I asked if he would start the job if I worked like two men. His eyes gleamed and we set the date.

I'd never worked in a sawmill before, but it was pretty straightforward. My jobs were at the front and back end: first to get the logs ready for the saw carriage and then to get rid of the slabs as they were sliced from the logs. I couldn't believe how heavy white oak is and John watched me as I struggled with the pieces as they came off, but he never once had to slow down. I took the first load home that night. Jack was there bright and early the next morning, anxious that these might not have been the white oak I was promised. As he set out to begin marking the timbers, he described them as "outstanding."

Ann's parents were following our adventures from England. They were clearing their attic when they came upon a Fabergé egg. Ann's great-grandfather was an international lawyer in Belgium who had a great fondness for art nouveau. He made a fortune and spent it supporting these artists. Ann's father is decidedly more temperate and believed the greatest value in such objects was their monetary one. He had spent the previous year having fun taking

things he thought worthless to the auction houses in London and selling them. He thought he'd cleared away anything of value when he came upon the egg and decided to sell it to distribute the money to his three children. It was sold in Switzerland for a fabulous sum and our portion came to 6,800 Swiss francs, which, converted to Canadian dollars, became $6,400. When our barn was finished in December of 1979, its total cost was almost exactly that amount.

We started framing on September 9 and had an old-fashioned barn raising on October 12 (our Canadian Thanksgiving weekend) with neighbors and friends. We started at ten and the barn frame was completed by four. Each day for the next week I'd look out the window to see that our barn was really standing there. It seemed too good to be true. It was magic, sheer magic.

The week after our roof was on the barn, the local doctor stopped in. He had been following my progress with interest and amusement as he drove his rounds. He raised sheep, and he held a young lamb in his arms, one that he and his wife had been saving for us. Apparently this was a lamb whose mother I'd saved while visiting his farm when she had difficulty lambing. I showed him that the barn was not really set up for sheep yet but he said that I needn't worry. Sheep don't really wander from home, he said. A few bales of hay would stop her from running out and she'd be fine. We now had our first sheep.

The next morning she was gone. With the fresh snowfall I could track her movements but got hopelessly turned around in her countless crisscrossings. After nearly four hours I gave up the search. Was this a harbinger of the future? That evening a neighbor drove up, wondering if we'd lost a sheep. His son had been out checking his trap lines and saw what he thought was a wolf caught in the fence, only to discover that it was the lamb instead. Relieved, I picked her up and brought her into the basement, where she lived for the next five months.

FLEECING THE LAMB

Ann's mother, who lived in England, had hurt her back and was bedridden. The news caused Ann much distress, and she felt that it would be good for us to be near and for her mother to meet her new grandchild, Stephanie, whom we had adopted the previous year. Ann had come across a teaching exchange program that would allow us to go to Britain, and although the application form said it might take up to four years for approval, we soon got word that our exchange was scheduled for September! We would be going to Tain, in the northeast of Scotland. We had three months to put our farming activities on hold for a year. I boarded our sheep at another farm and we bought transatlantic boat tickets for August.

I worked for most of the year away, first on a farm owned by the Duchess of Westminster, and then at a pipe coating plant. Working with sheep and cattle on the farm gave me the experience I was lacking. We weren't far from Inverness, then the capital of knitting in Great Britain. The teachers at Ann's school knitted during their school breaks, making it the perfect place for Ann to learn to knit. Everyone got sweaters as she learned her first Fair Isles, the Icelandic yoke sweaters. She even made her first sweater a cardigan by cutting it up the center, as the pattern said to do, all the while hoping that the pattern was right and the sweater wouldn't fall apart! (All those hours of knitting put to waste!) Of course it didn't (and doesn't) fall

apart, but you have to try it yourself to know for sure. I remember watching her as she struggled to pick up the band, doing it over and over again until the tension was right at last. It seemed to take forever and was such a frustrating experience.

Ann also learned to spin, working both with wool and other fibers. After each lesson she'd come home with a tiny ball of homespun yarn, enough maybe to knit the cuff of a sweater. It's unbelievable how many hours are spent spinning enough wool to make a sweater. But they are wonderfully satisfying, soul-fulfilling hours of watching the tent of carded wool spin into yarn.

When we returned to Canada the next summer, we were ready to begin farming. I finished building the barn, and our flock, now grown to eleven, came back that September. I thought we should start slowly, eventually building to a flock of fifty ewes. Fifty ewes would bring us 120 lambs per year, enough to pay for our basic living expenses. A ten-acre pasture, which

we had, would support that number of animals.

The sheep apprenticeship program I'd been in stressed out-of-season breeding. A normal lambing period is in March and April. The low levels of light in the fall, the cool temperatures, and the lush fall grasses bring the ewes into heat, leading to March/April lambing periods. The lambs are sold to market in September/October, which is, unfortunately, when both consumer demand and price is at its lowest. The two peak consumer periods for lamb are the Christmas and Easter seasons, but that is when supply of fresh lamb is lowest, too. Out-of-season breeding seeks to have the ewes bred sooner, or later, than their normal cycle dictates, linking their maturity to market demand. I designed our barn to provide the optimum light and temperature variables to induce the ewes to this cycle. Then, by varying their diets, I could get them ready to be bred.

I think there's a rule in farming that things will go wrong with even the best-laid plans. The first ewes we bought had what was thought to be a rare disease, and I had to sell my entire flock for slaughter. I'd nonetheless had my first lambing experience with them, and when all the costs were in we had broken even. Financially, that seemed very positive. We now knew that if we could manage to get the ewes to breed out of season and every eight months, a plan called accelerated lambing, our goals for the farm would be easily met.

Dorset sheep are particularly good at breeding out of season. They were originally developed for milking and have a down-style wool, thick with lots of crimp and bounce. It was perfect for making the types of sweaters we liked, arans and Fair Isles. I planned to milk the Dorsets and make cheese, using our root cellar to age it. When the time came to buy more sheep, we purchased twenty-seven ewe lambs that had been bred out of season. Those who lambed in four months would prove to be our most productive ewes. Those who didn't lamb then would be bred again to lamb four months later.

Our new sheep were wonderful. They produced excellent lambs and wool. We kept back a few fleeces from our first clip for Ann to spin and she set about making yarn for a sweater for her brother. I sold the rest to the local cooperative with high expectations. This was ideal wool, and they promised to pay top dollar for good wool. Five months later our check arrived for $.32 a pound. That was outrageous. It cost $.70 a pound just to shear the sheep, much less produce a fine fleece. And these had been fine fleeces.

I took our lambs to Toronto where the representative from the co-op had a shop and I talked to him about this. He felt that there had to have been a mistake made and that things would be different the next year. Not so. The third year we sold our wool to another source who paid us $.50 a pound; not much of an improvement. It just didn't seem right.

In that period, I'd begun to sell more of our lambs locally and dis-

covered that this was far more satisfying than trucking to Toronto. A local grocery store began buying, at first one lamb a month and then a lamb a week. Others added their names to our list and we sold most of our lambs from the farm. On my last trip to Toronto I topped the market and decided to celebrate.

Ann had continued to card and spin fleece, but it took so long to get enough wool to knit a sweater. She'd learned to knit with Icelandic wool and really enjoyed knitting, much more so than spinning. On this day I drove downtown after selling the lambs and went into a yarn shop, which now sells our wool. I noticed a sign on the counter that offered a 20 percent discount if I bought $200 worth of wool. I calculated all the sweaters Ann might knit and bought that amount of yarn.

I now had a four-hour drive home. It didn't take me long to realize that I had just spent $22 a pound for this yarn, on sale, when I had gotten only $.32 a pound for my fleece. I tried every calculation and scenario possible to work out

why this had to be so and could think of nothing that justified it. It seemed totally obscene to me, and I made the determination that I would find a better way. My experience of selling lamb locally convinced me that farmers can only improve the price they receive for their products if they take an active role in marketing them.

In theory, one could withhold wool from the market in a year when $.32 a pound is the best price on offer and wait for demand and price to rise. But the longer wool is kept off the market, the more likely it is to deteriorate in value. It is a classic dilemma.

At $.32 or $.50 a pound, I was the victim of "value lost." I needed to find a way to add value to my wool. If I could have my fleece made into yarn and take the yarn to market, surely I would stand a better chance of making a profit, or at least of not losing so much money. Just how I would go about marketing the yarn, I really had no idea. But I was determined to go forward. If nothing else, Ann would have lots of wool to knit!

THIS IS WOOL?

I SPENT THE WINTER of 1984 trying to find someone who would spin my wool into yarn. Before the wool is spun, it must be washed, and in commercial washing, the natural lanolin is often removed with astringent detergents. Without its lanolin, the wool is more likely to take on water. Since I worked outside building and farming in all weather, it made sense to me that I should keep the natural lanolin in the wool because it would then stay drier. I hadn't known what a complicating factor this would be. Only one of the places I contacted wrote back, a small family mill in Prince Edward Island. They sent me their price chart with samples of the colors I could have made. They would do everything from washing the wool to making the yarn. That was great, except that they wanted $1.20 a pound to wash the wool.

Any fool can wash wool, I thought. So when our next shearing was done I saved about half my fleece (one hundred pounds or so) to get spun into yarn. I waited until Ann had gone to school and carried the wool down to the washing machine. I figured that's what washing machines are for, but something told me Ann might have other ideas, so I decided to experiment on my own. I soaked the wool in warm water, loosening the dirt and grease, added mild detergent, rinsed until there were no more suds and brought the wool onto the front lawn to dry. Ann returned home from school. She was never sure what she'd find on

our lawn, and this was quite a sight. But the wool had washed beautifully and was almost dry. It had lost nearly half its weight from washing out the dirt and grease. I packed it in boxes and sent it off to the mill.

Then it struck me. Ann still hadn't knitted all the wool I'd bought two years ago, and we were about to get fifty more pounds of yarn. It wasn't reasonable to expect Ann to knit sweaters for everyone, much as she might like to. I was going to have to sell the yarn. Suddenly I was very nervous: how do you sell fifty pounds of yarn? Ann talked about our yarn at school. Whenever anyone bought a lamb from us, I made sure to mention our yarn. Everyone was interested. We all waited. It seemed to take forever. Then it arrived.

It was so much nicer than we'd expected. It wasn't itchy or scratchy. I'd never worn wool before that didn't prickle in one way or another. I thought that was just the way wool was. Could this be right? I thought about our lambs. Their wool wasn't itchy. Nor were the ewes when I handled them. Sheep's wool was as soft as could be. It never occurred to me to wonder why wool sweaters should

be itchy. But this wool wasn't. I showed it to everyone. Three weeks later, it was almost all sold, with only enough saved to knit a sweater for me. Even better, when I tallied all our expenses, I had made $2.35 a pound just by selling the wool myself.

It's not that any farmer will get rich selling fleece for $2.35 a pound. In our case, we'd get about $400 a year for our fleece, peaking at about $600 when we had our full complement of fifty ewes. What it meant was a psychological victory. I had turned a losing farm enterprise into a profitable one. I was on a roll! The following year I sent most of my fleece to the mill and made $2.65 a pound, economizing by using coffee bags instead of boxes. That avoided the "oversize package penalty" charged by the post office. We also made one other change.

After I washed the wool so wonderfully the previous year, Ann noticed that the washing machine was draining in a funny way; in fact, hardly at all. She asked me if I had any idea what the problem was. She thought I'd used some laundry tubs to wash the wool, as she had done, but I had to confess that I'd used the machine. It was probably the wool grease that was clogging the drains, I said. I took the machine apart and sure enough, the drainpipes were truly clogged. Suddenly $1.20 a pound to get the wool washed in the mill seemed pretty reasonable after all. I decided to contact the mill in Prince Edward Island again.

WOOLY THINKING

*I'*d often talked with John, my shearer, as he went about his specialized work. Occasionally I would help him shear, although I was never very good at it. But the activity gave us lots of time to talk about wool and the inequities of the marketplace. He told me about a major study done by the Ontario Sheep Association and the provincial government. Their conclusion was that there was nothing to be done about wool prices: even if farmers were paid nothing for their fleece, it would still be impossible to develop a viable woolen industry in the province.

Yet my own experience showed otherwise. My view was that we sheep farmers had to market our goods actively by ourselves, and if we did so, we'd be well rewarded. I talked with groups of farmers about this, but most were afraid to venture into the marketplace. Farmers generally wholesale their fleece to a variety of jobbers and cooperatives and never make contact with the mill, let alone the market. The advantage of going through a jobber or co-op is that the farmer gets rid of the wool quickly. Keeping it around is a nuisance for most. It's bulky, requires high and dry storage, the huge bags are awkward to maneuver, and they're always in the way. It's a lot of hard work, and thus the farmer is motivated to move the wool out quickly. The downside, however, is that the farmer loses money selling it to jobbers or co-ops for only $.32 to $.50 a pound, especially because sheep must be shorn regularly,

and shearing costs around $.70 a pound.

The more research I did, the more excited I became. During the American Civil War, farmers were paid $2.00 a pound for their fleece, compared with the $.32 to $.50 a pound we were getting. If the market could support those prices back then, surely our markets could now. After a year of talking and reading and thinking, I hit upon the solution in a conversation with

John, the shearer. If I could increase my income just by staying involved in my wool through the cleaning and dyeing processes, and by putting wool into sacks instead of boxes, there must be other inefficiencies in what I was doing. If I could find those things and fix them, I was willing to gamble that I could pay farmers four times or more what the market was paying them for their fleece and still develop a successful business.

It seemed incredible! The logic seemed inescapable. And yet, we'd all experienced kitchen-table economics that turned out to be missing some essential fact or set of variables that turned wished-for profits into losses. I felt that there was only one way to discover what those variables might be. I asked John if he would help me select good, clean fleeces as he was shearing at other farms. I would begin buying them.

Two things I had read led me to know that farmers really could be paid substantially more for their fleeces and not upset the market. One key lies in the cleanliness of the fleece presented to the mill. If the fleece is clean when it goes to the mill, the mill has to do less work washing it, and should therefore be able to charge less. The farmer should get paid a higher price for raising clean wool.

The second key is the way the wool market "thinks" and works. For example, in 1985, there was virtually no domestic manufacturing or retail market for the two million pounds or so of wool from

Canada. You simply couldn't sell it here; it was gotten rid of by the jobbers and co-ops who paid $.32 or $.50 a pound for it and exported it abroad, presumably for considerably more. Yet in that same year, Canada imported the equivalent of eighty-five million pounds of wool as finished goods! In other words, there was domestic consumer demand for over forty times the amount of wool being produced in Canada. How could the studies say there was no market? Perhaps they should have said there was no marketing, and hardly any manufacturing here in Canada.

I realized that if I were to sell every scrap of wool this country produces to Canadians as finished goods or packaged wool, the total Canadian wool production would amount to less than about 3 percent of the real market demand here. It was utter madness to believe that we could not develop markets here for our wool. How could I fail? How could anyone fail?

I talked with one of the participants of the provincial study and explained my ideas about enhancing values for the farmers. As she listened and questioned, she too thought it might work. If I could earn $2.65 a pound by selling my clip as yarn, it should be possible to pay farmers $2.00 a pound and put the other $.65 toward operating the company.

Transportation is a large part of the expenses in a woolen business: wool takes up a lot of space and is relatively light. Finished yields from commercial sources are as low as 35 percent; in other words, after the wool is washed and spun, the finished product weighs five to

six ounces for every pound of fleece the farmer ships to the commercial mill. That means a lot of money is spent trucking waste in the form of dirt and grease to mills around North America. If I could find a way to convince farmers to sell us super clean fleece, trucking costs could be dramatically reduced.

Washing costs are also based on

the incoming weight at the mill. High yielding, clean fleece would be lighter and so reduce that cost too. If we could encourage farmers to practice techniques that would result in super clean fleece, the savings in transportation and washing costs alone could provide us with the additional costs of running this business.

Then there is the question of moisture. No one quite realizes how much water wool will hold. My shearer told me the story of a local producer who wanted to prove the point. Before one of his sheep was shorn, they held her and poured a quart of water slowly over the center of her back where they'd parted the wool. Not a drop of water reached the ground; the wool soaked it all up. They then sheared the sheep and the wool didn't even feel very wet. Yet that fleece weighed more, the weight of a quart of water more!

I figured that if farmers could deliver dry, clean, high yielding fleece to me, I could reward them by paying a much better price for their wool than the jobbers and co-ops were paying. I would base the price I paid them on the weight of the finished wool that their shipment yielded after it was washed and dried. That price would vary according to how clean and high yielding their shipment was when it came to me and to the mill. But the chances were excellent that the price I could pay would be many times higher than what the wool market offered them.

And so I prepared for John the shearer to call with word of some select fleeces he'd shorn.

THE FIRST CALL came in early January of 1986. John had just shorn a farmer's wool and, being impressed with the quality, told him he should bring it to me. I hadn't given much thought to where I'd store wool if I bought some. I decided to store it in the log cabin. But I had to weigh it first, and the weigh scales were in the barn, two hundred yards away. But we'd had a heavy snowfall; we couldn't drive the load out there. So we loaded the bags, one at a time, onto a toboggan, dragged them to the barn and through the narrow front door, weighed them, and dragged them back to the log cabin. Oh, my back! Philosopher's Wool, as the enterprise had become known, did not seem like such a bright idea just then!

Cati, our oldest daughter, had her bedroom on the second floor of the log cabin, her dream home. Suddenly, her entrance started to fill with wool. One farmer happened to drive through a rain shower on his way with a load and we had to unpack his fleeces to let them dry out. Cati came back late that night to discover clouds of fleece covering the entrance to the cabin and her bedroom.

I added a lean-to to the drive shed and began storing the wool there. What an improvement that made, at least until we completed the job of turning the log cabin into our own retail outlet. We opened our store in the cabin with its newly finished interior the summer Cati went to art school in Cambridge. We are in a remote part of Ontario. I didn't actually believe we'd get many customers out where we were, but I did think that yarn shop owners would be anxious to come out to our showroom and see the wool in its natural setting. I was to be proven wrong on both counts: shop owners didn't come, but customers did.

By the time Cati returned from England, our yarn inventory had swollen to about eight hundred pounds, and her bedroom had become storage central for the wool coming back from the dyeing plant. She soon gave up hope of recovering her room and went on to university instead.

Our small successes were the source of other problems. As Philosopher's Wool developed, our friends in Prince Edward Island at the dyeing plant were worried that they might not be able to keep up with washing the volume of wool. It turned out that they too were using washing machines, commercial ones of course, and drying the wool over racks. They suggested I try to find a washing mill. I did. It was a blanket mill in Lachute, Quebec. After six months of negotiations as we dealt with one perceived problem after another, they

agreed to wash our wool. A friend drove the first load of twenty-five hundred pounds up to them.

At about this time, we were looking to buy a new vehicle. I had a big station wagon that was fine for hauling sheep and lambs around, but it was none too practical for hauling boxes and bags of wool. We bought a minivan. Twenty-five hundred pounds of raw wool was too much to fit in the minivan on its way to Quebec, but it seemed to me that after the wool lost 50 percent of its weight (in dirt, oil, and moisture washed and dried from the fleece, the norm in the cleaning and drying process) the washed lot should fit.

My father came along for the ride. He had his doubts. We made it to the mill where I explained that I'd come to pick up the wool. The men there looked at my van, looked at one another, and

shrugged their shoulders. If I said so, they said, and led us to the bin with our wool. They rolled over in laughter as they saw the look on my face. I couldn't believe it! "Impossible," I said! I would need three or four minivans to take all that wool with me. "One moment," they exclaimed, and came back with some bag clips. "You'll need these to shut the bags." My dad was busy filling the bags with wool, maybe just to rub it in!

After some negotiation and much more laughter, the mill agreed to bale the wool and ship it to the dyeing plant in Prince Edward Island. That was great. And when they got it in Prince Edward Island, they said it was perfect. What a wonderful feeling. We could now get wool washed, baled, and spun into yarn. Now we just needed to figure out retailing and wholesaling!

TO MARKET, TO MARKET . . .

ALL OF THE infrastructure of a small sheep-to-yarn company was in place. The only thing missing was sales. And that was a problem. Selling wool is different from selling lamb. With lamb, I was dealing with local customers. But selling wool means traveling from store to store and convincing them to buy. Ann and I set up a color line. I wanted the duller colors that are so traditional. Contemporary, vivid colors were too outlandish for my tastes, and I wanted to develop a heathery color line that more represented my background. We began with the blue, green, brown, and natural heathers, filling them in with colors from a large, modern mill just down the road from us.

I had talked with that mill a year or so earlier about the possibility of dyeing wool for us. The owner said it was a pity we didn't have washed wool, because they could then spin for us, as well. I talked with the owner's son, who said he really admired what I was trying to do. They'd tried finding a way of buying local wool and couldn't do so for two reasons: wool was so cheap on global markets, and they could not find a way to get wool washed. They were delighted I'd found a way and would work with us, even when it meant working what for them were very small lots. Their dyemaster is wonderful and spends lots of time helping us work out new colors. The only selling tool we had was a poster idea we were developing to promote Ontario wool. It was to be a picture of me with our sheepdog

Scruff and a baby lamb in a snow-covered field. Its slogan says: "Bring our shepherds in from the cold—Ontario wool, good for ewe, good for us all."

Ann was still teaching and I was the primary homemaker. Once or twice a week, I would have an opportunity to become the traveling salesman. My problem, however, was that I didn't know where the wool stores were. There was a large chain headquartered near Kitchener-Waterloo, and I made an appointment to see them.

On a miserable, cold December day with blowing snow and icy roads, I took our entire inventory of yarn in the old station wagon and headed out to the city. I talked with the president and his father. They agreed to try selling our yarn in their store. I was elated. On the way home I had a great idea. 1986 was a time of farm crisis stories,

with many farms shut down by the banks that held their loans. Land and commodity prices had declined radically, and farmers, most of whom were current with their debt, were still forced to repay large sums of money to the banks to compensate for the falling value of their assets. This was impossible for most, and there were farm foreclosures everywhere. I decided to phone the business editor of the newspaper in Kitchener, *The Record*, to tell him about this good-news farm story.

The editor wrote a wonderful story about Philosopher's Wool and then asked me if I would go back to the store for a photo shoot. I was delighted. That is how I met Philip Walker, the photographer of this book and of our sweaters. We hit it off immediately. I described a poster I wanted to make, and he said that he hoped I didn't have a photographer for it. He wanted to be our photographer! It didn't matter that we couldn't afford to pay him; he was happy to trade a lamb for his services, an exchange rate we've used many times since. We waited for the perfect snowy day and he drove out the hundred miles through miserable weather just so we could get the pristine view we needed.

I wanted the poster message to convey the idea that ordinary people can make a difference to farmers if only they can make a choice in their purchases. The article in *The Record* supported this view: two magazines had phoned to write stories about Philosopher's because they'd seen this article. I realized that there were people sympathetic to this message. And I realized that no matter how Philosopher's Wool grew in time, its products must remain affordable to ordinary, working people because they understand and are sympathetic to the difficulties of making a living. If we could supply these folks with high quality wool at affordable prices I was convinced they would buy our yarns.

Still, Philosopher's Wool had to find ways to get through the maze of advertising and messages that assault people every day. We had to present our products more skillfully. Showing the quality of our wool in finished products, like sweaters, was, we felt, the best way.

Initially, I didn't realize we'd need our own sweater patterns. Weren't there lots of patterns anyway? Why should we make more? I thought that if I could demonstrate to the stores how much nicer the sweaters were when made from our yarn, they'd happily abandon the others and sell ours. I'd buy a pattern book or two and on my next visit, show them something knit with our wool. It wasn't long before one of the stores pointed out that we really shouldn't be doing this; these patterns belonged to other yarn manufacturers who design them to sell their own yarns. We would have to develop our own patterns if we wanted to sell our wool through stores.

What an incredibly exciting idea! Imagine the freedom of designing your own sweaters. I wondered why we hadn't thought of this ourselves. Ann was still

teaching school, and a number of the parents of her students were knitters. They began knitting sweaters for us. At first, we modified existing designs, trying to clear up problems we encountered knitting these other patterns. But soon we had our first pattern, modeled on the Icelandic yoke sweaters.

We'd noticed that these sweaters often bulged pattern-wise as the sweater decreased to the neck. We created what looked like a raglan-sleeved sweater. We played with adding stripes around the chest in complementary colors. It was a really lovely, simple, pullover sweater, and very popular.

But research and development took time and were expensive and resulted in a new problem. It was well and good to be designing and knitting these sweaters. But without sales, revenues were getting short. Our store had proven to be a popular venture during the summer, giving us lots of revenue to go on knitting. But once summer ended, our source of revenues ended and we were now coming into late fall. What should we do? We had lots of wool and lots of sweaters, but less and less capital.

Just when things looked completely bleak, there was a knock at the log cabin. Three corporate lawyers had been walking in the Inverhuron Provincial Park next door to our farm and had lost their way. They asked if they could use our phone. Of course they could.

The first one in the door saw the piles of sweaters we had on the floor, roughly separated according to color tone. He was amazed. Did we sell these, he wanted to know, and which pile could he buy? I assured him he could buy whichever pile he liked, and that was that. They made their phone calls, found their way, and were gone, leaving us with enough money to go on knitting and designing for another month.

COLOR YOUR OWN

$\mathcal{S}$OMEONE FROM the National Ballet of Canada came to our store. Did I, she wondered, know of their "Sugar Plum Fair," held in a faux castle in Toronto just before Christmas, and would I be interested in buying a booth to sell our sweaters at this fair? The booths cost a lot, but the ballet used the profits to sponsor dance students. I studied modern dance and was excited about the possibility of supporting dance this way. I also wondered whether our sweaters were good enough for this upscale market and felt that this was the best way to find out. So we applied and were given a booth in a prime location.

Unfortunately, the booth was a long, narrow, sideways triangle, rather than the normal rectangular shape usually given. This shape certainly had its advantages. It gave us a long aisle exposure, but it completely lacked depth. We were really struggling with how to set up our display when Ann came up with the idea of putting folding sweater racks along the back wall. I headed off to a neighbor who had a small woodworking shop, and we made a pair of basswood folding racks with doweling to display the sweaters. We set up our display in the log cabin. It worked perfectly, and we were ready to go.

I thought we should bring kits to match the sweaters. There might be people who would like to knit the sweaters instead of buying them. This would be an affordable alternative for knitters, especially for those who had more time than

money. Ann was set against the idea. She insisted that kits would never work out quite right. I countered that we would put in more wool and make bigger kits. In the end, we did put together kits and they were a resounding success at this show. People loved the idea of making these sweaters. They were thrilled, or so they thought, with the idea of mixing up the colors themselves. It made such perfect sense when they were standing in front of our booth. We also sold lots of finished sweaters; some people were buying two or three at a time. We left the show amazed with our success.

The kits not only created a great product line, they solved a problem, something that might otherwise have been seen as a flaw with Philosopher's Wool yarns. You see, no two sheep have exactly the same color wool. Sometimes the differences are slight, but sometimes they can be quite pronounced. Since we neither bleach our wool, nor strip it of its natural grease,

each sheep's contribution of wool is a different shade of off-white to off-yellow. As well, every dye lot is always a little different from the last. In the case of Philosopher's Wool yarns, those differences were occasionally quite noticeable. We'd begun to build up a substantial quantity of "odd" dye lots. Sweater Kit One, our first, allowed us to use the occasional "odd" skein, but it was like a drop in the ocean.

What Ann had enjoyed most about the Icelandic sweaters was their Fair Isle design. Their third color, however, was a real pain. As she looked through books of traditional Fair Isle motifs, she came to the conclusion that it was entirely unnecessary. She's always had a great fondness for miniatures and was really taken with the peeries, the smaller bands that separate the major motifs. Playing with a number of these led to "Tradition," one of our first and certainly one of our most successful Fair Isle patterns. As well, our daughter had just had our first grandchild, and Ann had to knit a sweater for her. While "Tradition" used four or five colors in eleven skeins, the "Jenna Louise" (as it came to be called) used odds and ends of wool left over from other projects.

The next summer at our store, everyone wanted to kit a "Jenna Louise" as an adult sweater, and "Color Your Own" was born. This sweater solved all our old dye lot problems: it took three skeins of the main color and any seven or eight other colors. And it made each Philosopher's sweater unique: no two knitters would have the exact same color combinations or shadings.

The "one of a kind" nature of our sweaters was a major selling point at the shows, but a bit of an issue after the fact. We have always made a point of putting our phone number on our patterns, so that we can help people who might be having difficulty. Most of our early kit sales were at our store, where we had plenty of time to show each customer how to mix colors. At a show, things are so much busier and not everyone gets enough time. So after each show, our phone was busy for the next couple of weeks as customers opened their kits only to discover that we meant what we'd said: we don't tell you where to put colors. It is such a thorough shock. Each person is convinced that it is impossible to get a sweater as beautiful as the one at the show. It was that one they wanted to knit and mixing up the colors would only make the sweater different. Couldn't we tell them where the colors on the sweater kit they'd just bought should go?

We'd explain the concept again that it is really unnecessary to know precisely where the colors go; it only matters that all the colors are used. It's not a perfect match that's successful, but the sum total of the colors. For example, if you look at a natural setting that is strikingly lovely, it's not because the colors are exactly the same as the last beautiful bit of scenery you saw. Each setting has its own random combination of complementary colors that makes it so captivating

and special. The same is true with our sweaters.

We eventually came up with the idea of using dice. Customers would use them first to select the color and then again to select the number of rows of that color before changing. Start with the sleeves, we'd remind the knitter, because in a small piece like a sleeve, the progression of colors is so much faster and you see the effect much sooner. When people started phoning us to tell us that they didn't really want to throw the dice any more, we responded by telling them that they'd graduated! What a wonderful feeling. They were each so excited at what they'd created. When two or three would show up at a later event wearing the same sweater and colorway, with each sweater different from the other, but each beautiful in its own

right, customers fully understood the concept. "It was such a liberating experience," they told us. "We were no longer entrapped in someone else's notion of what's appropriate. We could trust ourselves."

The key is the colorways themselves, which have expanded and become more attuned over the years. As things are now, each of our colors can be used in combination with ten or more other colors, giving us great flexibility in creating the groupings we call colorways. Each colorway consists of between eleven and eighteen colors, allowing us to create patterns that look remarkably different from one another simply by changing the colorway. At a show, our booth will typically have no more than six or seven of our sweater patterns. Everyone is continuously surprised that there are so few patterns present, yet impressed by the variety of our sweaters. The differences are in the combinations of colors.

Our experience at The Sugar Plum Fair whetted our appetite for such shows; they are truly exciting. They expose us to a wide audience, and that audience is brutally honest. If everyone walks by your booth without stopping, it's obvious that something is terribly wrong and changes need to be made. On the other hand, if your booth is busy, you know that people are excited about your work. We'd joined a trade association and displayed our sweaters in a booth at their wholesale show. Everyone was impressed with our work, and we were invited to join their show circuit that had us crisscrossing Canada.

TRANSMISSION BLUES

*P*HONED THE blanket mill in Lachute to have them wash more wool. "Did no one tell you," they asked, "that we are no longer washing wool?"

"But it was only a couple of months ago that you washed the first batch. It was perfect."

"Sorry; too bad," they said.

"This can't be," I thought. I explained that the mill in Ontario could do the work for me only if I supplied them with well-washed wool. "You have to wash at least one more batch," I explained to them. "If I promise to have it there this week, couldn't you do so? And do you know any other mills that could wash wool for us?" Yes, they would wash the wool for me; no, they didn't know anywhere I might get wool washed. I sent the load.

Now what was I going to do for a washing mill? I phoned everyone I could think of, each conversation leading to other contacts. I found mills as far away as Texas that eventually lead me to two closer mills, the one in Rhode Island, the other in Pennsylvania. In the end, I selected the mill in Pennsylvania, the largest top-hat maker in North America. They have been washing our wool ever since.

I liked the idea of having to travel to the U.S. to wash our wool. I enjoy traveling. As well, the new relationship with the Pennsylvania mill made our little business an international one. I bought a 1973 GMC pick-up and a trailer. The pick-up had 414,000 miles on it at the time, and I put on another 75,000 miles before it started to fall

apart. One year we used seven transmissions hauling the wool through the mountains of Pennsylvania, following the Susquehanna River from its origins. I often fantasized about loading the wool onto a barge and floating down the river to Harrisburg before heading to Philadelphia. The whole enterprise made me feel as if I were a medieval merchant traveling to foreign climes to make my fame and fortune.

But the reality of the situation had its bumps. Customs officers at the U.S./Canada border were often confused by the differences in weight between the load of wool I brought into the States and the load I brought back. I might arrive at U.S. customs with papers that said I was bringing in a load that weighed, say, four thousand pounds. By the time the mill had finished washing out the grease and dirt and drying the excess

moisture, the return weight was listed as only twenty-five hundred pounds. "What did you do with the other wool?" the customs folks would ask. Even differences between the humidity at the weigh-in location in Canada and the humidity at the mill in Philadelphia would cause a variation of twenty or thirty pounds or more. U.S. and Canadian customs officers often had to learn more about wool than they had ever dreamed of learning. Eventually, I was able to obtain official papers, which helped ease the border issues for the next seven years.

We made up to five trips a year like this. And there wasn't a trip that didn't lead to one challenge or another. Once, I drove thirty-one hundred pounds of wool through a hurricane. By the time I arrived in Philadelphia, the wool was soaked and the load weighed close to eight thousand pounds. It drained for three weeks at the mill. The mill workers even wondered if they would need to wash the wool at all.

And there were those truck transmissions: the original transmission lasted sixteen trips. Between the next two trips I had used six transmissions. Something wasn't right! I was constantly breaking down and invariably kind people on the freeways and highways would stop to help me out. The trip before I encountered the hurricane was somewhat typical.

I had been driving from a farm in eastern Ontario, where I picked up my last load, to a border crossing when the transmission slipped.

I ignored it. It slipped again. "Can't be true," I thought, "this is the sixth one this year. It must be something else." I made it to a motel near the border. It was three in the morning.

I woke anxiously at seven, crossed the border, and headed off toward Pennsylvania. I drove for a couple of hours then left the turnpike and stopped for gas. I was exhausted. I filled the tank and started the truck. It wouldn't move. Transmission trouble.

"You can't leave that truck here," the man at the station said.

"It won't go," I said.

"You gotta move it," he said. "You're blocking my gas sales."

"What can I do?" I asked.

"You from Canada?" he asked.

"Yes, I am."

"Okay, let me make a couple of calls," he said.

Fifteen minutes later, a tow truck arrived. "Hop in," the driver said. "I'll fix you up." Off we went to his shop in the town of Leicester. I had Leicester sheep, along with my Dorset. "What seems to be the problem?" he asked. I recited my tale of loads too heavy for transmissions. "Nonsense," he said. "You've got a baby load for this truck. Did you know this truck has a Corvette engine?" I didn't. "Ya need a heavy-duty tranny ta match," he said.

We arrived at his garage. It took a while, but he lined up a replacement transmission. It was 11:30. Two other men put the truck on a jack hoist. "Do you mind if I take this trailer off?" he asked.

"Not at all."

"The transmission won't be here till three," he said. "I know a clean, cheap motel just down the road. Do you want me to take you there?"

"Of course," I said. I showered and slept like a baby. By five o'clock the new rebuilt transmission was in and I was ready to roll. I made eighteen more trips before I stopped using the truck. It was falling apart. But the "tranny" was still going strong.

The kindness of people will usually pull you through the worst of times. By now, many of our neighbors had taken a real interest in our enterprise, and many local ladies were knitting our sweaters for sale in our store or shows. While many exhibitors fly around the country, Ann and I prefer to drive to the shows, which means we're away from home for weeks at a time. When we went on the road, our knitters would look after our store and farm. I tried to organize our sheep so that there would be no lambing while we were away. It seemed simple enough to do. In order for sheep to breed, both the rams and the ewes have to be together for a while. I wanted to allow them "quality time," but only at certain times of the year. Thus, lambing would occur when we'd be home and when it would also work out best for marketing.

However, sheep have their own notions of what's right and wrong, and frequently enough, the rams would break down barriers to join with the ewes. The ewes didn't seem to mind, and I'd only discover the next morning what they'd been up to the previous night. By this time, considerable activity would have taken place and our knitters would be faced with newborn lambs during our trips.

Before we'd leave on a trip, knitters like Shirley or Sherry would demand to know whether the animals had been "up to no good." Now, being a philosopher, I would respond that they hadn't been doing a thing wrong. I strongly believe that breeding among sheep is a good and natural thing. At least, it is for them. Nothing wrong with it at all. Except that lambing always leads to more work. At properly scheduled lambing time, I would disappear to the barn with the animals for up to three weeks, leaving Ann to look after wool business alone. Our knitters, though, were only here one at a time. What with answering the phone and packing kits for our shows as well as helping the customers who increasingly drove one hundred miles or so to get to our store, things were busy enough without the addition of lambing.

Luckily our vets have been extraordinarily supportive, coming out any time lambing occurred. Besides, only a few ewes would lamb then, so the stress wasn't too great, and it's always such a great joy to see these newborns springing about once they find their feet. Anyway, the problem of handling the lambing while we were gone was solved when Cati introduced us to Tom, who has become Cati's husband and our son-in-law, a mainstay of the farm operation, and part of our lives. He takes care of lambing when I'm away. And he and Cati have presented us with three human lambs to boot, our first grandchildren.

MEMORIES ARE MADE OF THIS

*I*T WAS SEPTEMBER. Ann had managed to find another teacher who wanted to job share with her, each of them working full-time for half the year. Ann's portion began in mid-January. What a joy! It meant we could travel together, be Philosopher's Wool together.

The people who ran the wholesale show we had been in had just begun consumer shows, and wanted us to travel from one end of the country to the other with them. Of course, no one expected us to be mad enough to drive, but I love driving and thought this would be the opportunity of a lifetime. And indeed, that first year was mad. We had to drive to Vancouver for the first show, Winnipeg next, then Halifax for the third show before finishing in Calgary. We pored over maps wondering how we could possibly make the trip with each show on successive weekends. Like anything else, there's only one way to find out. Off we went.

Nothing would work if we couldn't get to Vancouver in four days, so there was no point leaving ourselves more than four days to get there. We had no idea just how expansive Canada is, nor how beautiful. Our plan was to share the driving.

Ann didn't like driving the van when it was loaded to the gills and she had to rely on the mirrors for side and rear visibility. We were in northern Ontario driving up to a small town when she noticed she was driving too fast. The person ahead of us was pulled over by the police and Ann sailed by, slowing down to the speed limit. In town we stopped for coffee; then I took over driving. The police were waiting for us and pulled me over.

"You were driving pretty fast coming into town, weren't you," the officer asked rhetorically. What could I say?

"Of course we were," I said, "and I was shocked to realize it. We

slowed down immediately," I added, explaining how upset I was to have been speeding in the first place, and that the road and its traffic seem to lull you into its own rhythm. "I wasn't speeding now, was I?" I asked.

"No," he said, "you weren't. We love our children here and would hate to see them in an accident because someone was speeding."

"You're absolutely right," I said.

"All right," he said, "go on."

No ticket. Ann was smiling broadly. "Imagine," she said, "you would have got the ticket when you weren't even the one driving."

As we drove, Ann played with some of the new designs she was planning and we'd talk about them together. At that time, I didn't knit, so when she drove, I'd just be watching the road. She didn't enjoy driving as much as she enjoyed knitting, and I didn't enjoy being a passenger as much as I enjoyed driving. So we made an arrangement that holds to this day. I would drive and she would knit and plan.

We made it to Vancouver with hours to spare. The show organizers were waiting expectantly for us. They couldn't believe we'd made it but were very pleased. Ann was scheduled to give her first classes in two-handed Fair Isle for them the next morning. All that was left was for us to set up our booth, and this went very smoothly.

Two years earlier someone from Vancouver had wanted to set up Philosopher's Wool West, doing for British Columbia producers what I was now doing for Ontario producers. We worked together and I bought the wool from farmers there and had it processed into

yarn for her. Unfortunately, she wasn't successful in selling it, so this would be an opportunity to help develop that market with her. We set up a spinning and shearing display in our booth with her guild and now stepped back to see what our booth looked like.

It was wonderful to behold. Sweaters were overflowing, fleeces

were on their way to becoming yarn, spinning wheels were ready, we were ready. The moment had come. Would anybody like us? That doubt plagues us at each show, as if we are throwing a party and are afraid no one will come. The minutes and seconds before the doors open drag on forever as we wait. And then the rush of the crowd, people milling around, looking, touching, and talking.

Ann's class was scheduled for eleven in the morning, and her students had come to check us out. They were amazed: could they really knit any of the sweaters on display with the two-handed technique Ann was going to teach? Everyone was skeptical. They went to Ann's class and returned an

hour later. They had learned the technique in less than an hour. Transformed, they looked at the sweaters, and then our sweater kits, with new eyes, many buying kits they couldn't believe they were buying. It was wonderful for all of us, like joining a secret society.

Over the course of the weekend the "buzz of the show" became Ann's two-handed method, especially weaving the color on the right hand while knitting with the left. It was round with the right, round with the left, undo the right and through. I started to dance the steps, tripping myself up when I undid the right. Others joined me and soon our whole booth was dancing this dance, chanting, "Round with the right, round with the left, undo the right, and through."

Alas, even a good dance has its limitations. People learned the method, bought our kits, and there was enthusiasm everywhere. Then they'd go home. The kit would sit in a bag. Weeks and months might go by before they started the kit. The only thing worse than not knowing how to do two-handed Fair Isle is knowing that you have done it once but now can't remember how.

We altered the classes: we gave longer ones, we gave hat classes, half-day classes, full-day classes. We'd teach continuously in our booth. By now I had learned to knit too, and I could even teach the method over the phone! Everyone loved Ann's classes. They left empowered, knowing they could actually do this, that it could really be done. They were convinced; they were believers! And then, time would pass and forgetfulness would set in. Not everyone, of course, but enough suffered forgetfulness that we knew we had to find another way to reinforce our teaching of this method.

We found the answer on the road. We began to plan the routing of our trips so that we could visit friends and drop in at stores that sold our wool. One of our friends, Bruce Steele, lives in Regina and was the host of an internationally syndicated television show, *What on Earth*. We showed Bruce our product and told him about our farm, and he decided to do a program segment with us. We set up our booth in the park outside his studio. The natural setting showed off our sweaters beautifully.

Bruce worked up the background for his interview with us by asking, among many other things, why our wool isn't itchy. He couldn't believe the comfort and softness of our socks and sweaters, and

decided the whole world had to know about our product. Ann insisted that the focal point of the show had to be the two-handed Fair Isle, while I, of course, thought that the important part was that farmers were being paid more for their fleece. Bruce accommodated each of us. It was fun working on the program, and for the first time we saw just how clearly the two-

handed method could be shown on television.

The popularity of this segment surprised all of us. Other media called and wanted to do stories. The next time we visited Bruce in Regina, we asked him about making a video, what it involved, and what it would cost. We watched other knitting videos and were convinced we could do better. Bruce was too, so we drew up a budget and a plan. With Bruce's director from *What on Earth* as cameraman and director, we set out to make a high-quality video that showed just how simple Ann's two-handed Fair Isle method is to learn and how simple it is to construct a sweater using it. We filmed the video on our farm and in the surrounding parklands, using the scenery as a backdrop for both the instruction and for our story. The finished product was nearly an hour long and looked lovely.

We tested it with our knitters. They said we had a hit. Now there could be no forgetting. The complete two-handed Fair Isle instruction was on tape, with camera angles of the knitting from the knitter's point of view.

We packaged it and took it out to the first shows. Would anyone buy it? They did. Those who bought a copy of the video on the first day of a show would often return to the show the next day, telling everyone who would listen how they too had to have a copy. We know this book will inspire you in the same way. Be free with your knitting. The simple structures Ann has given here will let you make the Fair Isle sweater of your dreams and will support the farmers who produce these fine fleeces.

PHILOSOPHER'S FAIR ISLE TECHNIQUES

TOOLS AND SUPPLIES

FAIR ISLE KNITTING is easy and very enjoyable when done using the simple techniques in this book. To create one of our sweaters, all you really need is the desire to knit, the yarn, and a circular needle to start your knitting; as you continue, the other tools and supplies will be handy to have. This book is about empowering you. With it, you will learn how simple and rhythmic any Fair Isle pattern can be.

Philosopher's Wool Yarn

We design our sweaters especially for our own Philosopher's Wool yarn, which is available in two different weights and a wide array of gorgeous colors. Our yarns will enable you to make vibrant sweaters that are soft and warm and hold their shape. They are virtually non-allergenic and certainly not scratchy or itchy. Most sweaters in this book call for a total of eleven skeins of yarn. Using three to six skeins in a main color and five to eight skeins in other colors, you can create rich visual effects in any of our patterns—and you never need to use more than two colors at any one time. We offer a distinctive palette of colors, ranging from traditional heathers and solid shades to unique "barbecued" wools and cool colors that are colored with powdered, unsweetened drink mixes. Philosopher's Wool yarns vary slightly in texture and thickness, which gives finished sweaters not only a hand-knit, but also a handspun look. For our complete palette, see "The Colorways," page 46. For information about ordering Philosopher's Wool yarn by mail or Internet, see "Resources," page 128. Our two-ply, worsted-weight, four-ounce skein has 175 to 275 yards, depending on the mill that spins the yarn, and knits up in Fair Isle work at 4½ to 5¼ stitches per inch. Our three-ply, chunky-weight, four-ounce skein has 120 to 180 yards and knits up in Fair Isle work at around 4 stitches per inch.

Knitting Needles

Nickel-plated knitting needles are smooth and slippery, which allows our wool yarn with the lanolin left in it to glide over them easily and makes your knitting go faster. Look for a circular needle that has smooth tips so you won't hurt your fingers as you knit. Double-pointed needles are best for starting children's sleeves, but for everything else, use a circular needle. Follow these guidelines for choosing the best needle sizes and lengths for your project.

You will also need a tape measure, access to a sewing machine, scissors, T-pins or safety pins, and two tapestry needles, one size 13 and one smaller one.

NEEDLES FOR TWO-PLY PHILOSOPHER'S WOOL YARN*

Sweater Size	Sleeves	Body	Ribbing
Adult	16" (40 cm) size 8 (5 mm) circular	32" (80 cm) size 8 (5 mm) circular	32" (80 cm) size 4 (3½ mm) circular
Child	16" (40 cm) size 8 (5 mm) circular and size 8 (5 mm) double-pointed (to begin)	24" (60 cm) size 8 (5 mm) circular	24" (60 cm) size 4 (3½ mm) circular

* You may need to use different-size needles to achieve the tension suggested in each pattern.

NEEDLES FOR THREE-PLY PHILOSOPHER'S WOOL YARN*

Sweater Size	Sleeves	Body	Ribbing
Adult	16" (40 cm) size 10½ (6½ mm) circular	32" (80 cm) size 10½ (6½ mm) circular	32" (80cm) size 7 (4½ mm) circular
Child	16" (40 cm) size 10½ (6½ mm) circular and size 10½ double-pointed (to begin)	24" (60 cm) size 10½ (6½ mm) circular	24" (60cm) size 7 (4½ mm) circular

*You may need to use different-size needles to achieve the tension suggested in each pattern.

THE SECRET TO FAIR ISLE SIMPLIFIED

*F*air Isle knitting produces beautiful, multicolored sweaters using only two colors at a time. Traditionally, two techniques have been popular for carrying a strand of yarn behind the stitches on a needle until it is needed again. *Stranding* is a method where the color that is not being knitted loops along behind the stitches on the needle. This results in a float, or loose strand of yarn that is carried behind two, three, four, or even five stitches, which can create puckering, as well as tangled or twisted yarn. *Twisting* is a technique where both colors of yarn are carried in one hand and twisted after alternate stitches. When the knitter twists the yarn alternately clockwise and counterclockwise, it does not tangle. This process produces a fine, woven fabric, but it requires a lot of wrist and finger movements.

Two-handed Fair Isle is a method in which each color is carried in one hand, as shown. This works very efficiently; you use your left hand to knit in the European (or German) style, and your right hand to knit in the North American (or British) style. We use four different stitches to achieve beautiful, flat knitted fabric, which appears woven on the inside. We want all knitters, from beginners to experienced, to have access to this method. You can master these stitches in just a few evenings, and they will make any Fair Isle project far quicker and easier. To practice this method, cast on about twenty-five to thirty stitches, knit three or four rows, and practice on this small swatch. Just practice on the knit side; you will not need to purl back. Because our sweaters are knitted on circular needles, the right side of your knitting always faces you and there is no need to purl.

Knitting is much easier if you anchor both strands of yarn on your little fingers, as shown below, before you start. This method of Fair Isle knitting really does take only about fifteen minutes to learn and two or three evenings to master. It can save you many hours over the course of your knitting career.

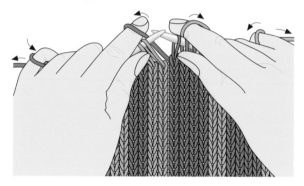

Knitting with the Color on Your Right Needle

Stitches #1 and #2 are knitted in the North American, or British, style. Stitch #1 is for every odd-numbered right-hand stitch. Stitch #2 is for every even-numbered right-hand stitch.

1. To knit Stitch #1, insert your right needle into the first stitch on your left needle. Bring the right-hand yarn around the right needle counterclockwise, as shown.

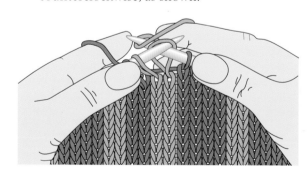

2. Bring the right-hand yarn through the loop on the left needle, as shown, and move the stitch to the right needle. This completes Stitch #1.

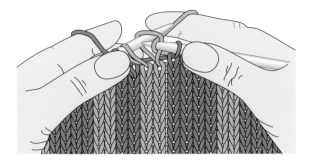

3. Stitch #2 carries the left-hand yarn behind a right-hand stitch. Insert your right needle into the next stitch on your left needle and under the left-hand yarn behind the left needle, as shown.

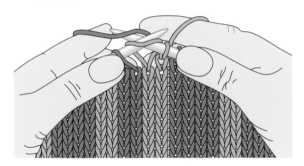

4. Bring the right-hand yarn around the right needle counterclockwise. Lift the left-hand yarn away and bring the right-hand yarn through the stitch on your left needle, as shown. Move the stitch to the right needle. This completes Stitch #2.

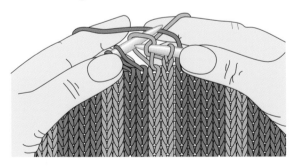

Tip

You should bring only the right-hand yarn through the stitch on your left needle. Do not allow the left-hand yarn to come through the stitch.

5. Continue alternating Stitch #1 and Stitch #2 several more times, until you feel comfortable knitting with the color on your right needle.

Knitting with the Color on Your Left Needle

Stitches #3 and #4 are knitted in the European, or German, style. Stitch #3 is for every odd-numbered left-hand stitch, and Stitch #4 is for every even-numbered left-hand stitch.

1. To knit Stitch #3, insert your right needle into the next stitch on your left needle, so that it goes behind your left-hand yarn from right to left, as shown.

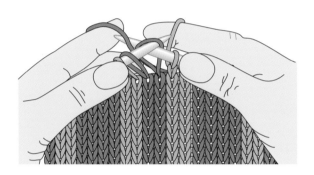

Tip

If you have twisted your knit stitch, your right needle was not behind your left-hand yarn.

2. Hook the left-hand yarn with your right needle, and bring it through the stitch on your left needle, as shown, and move the stitch to the right needle. This completes Stitch #3.

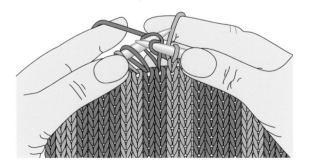

3. Stitch #4 carries the right-hand yarn behind a left-hand stitch. Insert your right needle into the next stitch on your left needle. Bring the right-hand yarn around the right needle counterclockwise, as shown. Do not knit the stitch; the yarn will be here only temporarily.

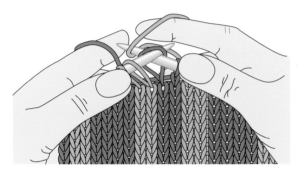

4. Lay your left-hand yarn right over the top of the right-hand yarn, so that both yarns are going in the same direction, as shown.

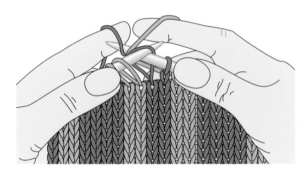

5. Bring the right-hand yarn around the right needle, this time in the opposite, or clockwise, direction, as shown. You have now removed it from the needle.

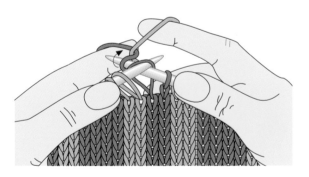

6. Using your right needle, hook the left-hand yarn and bring it through the stitch on your left needle, as shown, and move the stitch to the right needle. This completes Stitch #4.

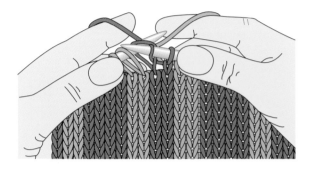

7. Continue alternating Stitch #3 and Stitch #4 several more times, until you feel comfortable knitting with the color on your left needle.

Introducing a New Color

You can change to a new color before the beginning of a row (where your row marker is, at the side of the body, or at the underarm seam of a sleeve), carrying it behind your work for about six stitches before you actually need to work with it. This means that any time you introduce a new color, you will be working with three strands of yarn for about twelve stitches. When you have finished your project, there will be virtually no ends to weave in.

1. Lay the new strand of yarn in your hand that is not knitting, and carry it behind your work until you are ready to use it. Move the new color from hand to hand as you change from left- to right-handed knitting and vice versa.

2. When you begin to knit in pattern with the new color, weave out the old color in the same way for about 6 stitches. Then cut it close to the surface of your knitting (about ½"). It is easier to change just 1 yarn color in any given round, but you can change both.

Tubular Knitting

*O*ur sweaters are drop-shouldered garments that are designed for knitting on a circular needle. Knitting in the round is wonderful for many reasons: there is no need to purl, your work always faces you, and it is easy to keep your pattern free of errors and avoid unraveling. Follow these easy steps to knit a two-handed Fair Isle pullover or cardigan that will be both beautiful and unique.

DETERMINING FIT

We include a wide range of sizes in our sweater patterns. Finished chest sizes range from 39" to 56". We find that the vast majority of people can wear a finished cardigan that has a 48" chest measurement, a sleeve length of 19" (21" for pullovers), and a 29" body length. Our sweaters are designed to measure 10" to 16" larger than actual chest size.

When you choose the size for the sweater you want to make, think about how you want the finished sweater to look. A sweater that is 10" larger than chest measurement will have a more fitted look, while a sweater with 16" of ease will look more casual. As a guide to calculating the dimensions you want in a finished sweater, measure a drop-shouldered sweatshirt or sweater that fits the wearer well. Lay the garment on a flat surface and measure the chest size, the sleeve length, the width at the top of the sleeve (or armhole depth),

and the total body length, as shown. Write down these measurements and keep them close at hand. After knitting the sleeves, where fit is not likely to be a problem, you will be able to measure your own knitting tension in the round and use it as the basis for determining which body size you should use for the size sweater you want to knit. If you need to make a garment smaller or larger than the sizes listed, you can reduce or increase the number of stitches for the ribbing and after the body ribbing by one or more full pattern repeats; for example, twelve stitches, or a multiple of twelve, for a "Tradition" sweater.

KNITTING THE SLEEVE TUBES

Our sweater sleeves are graduated tubes that start off with ribbed narrow cuffs knitted back and forth, followed by a Fair Isle tube that increases gradually to a comfortable width at the top. We recommend that you always start with the sleeves, for several reasons. Knitting a sleeve is an easy way to learn a Fair Isle pattern quickly, the first sleeve functions as an effective color map for knitting the second sleeve to match, and sleeves serve as a good swatch for measuring your own tubular knitting tension. ("Fin and Feather Together" is one exception to the rule. We recommend that you knit the body first when making that sweater.)

1. Cast on the number of stitches called for in your pattern and knit the ribbing, changing yarn colors as you like. See page 45 for ideas on where to change color. After you finish the ribbing, knit 1 round in your background color, increasing the number of stitches called for in your pattern before you start knitting the Fair Isle pattern.

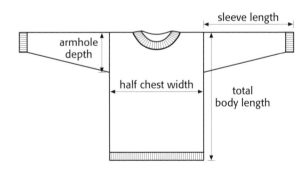

Tip

The sleeves in our patterns are loose enough that, no matter what your tension is, fit is not likely to be a problem. The suggested lengths of the sleeves are different in two- and three-ply patterns because the sweaters drape differently in the two weights.

2. After you knit a couple of inches above the ribbing, stop to check your work to make sure that the knitted fabric you are creating is neither too loose and sloppy, nor too tight and rigid. At this point, you can easily change to a different-size circular needle if necessary.

3. As you knit the sleeve tube, increase 1 stitch at both the beginning and the end of every fourth round for 2-ply yarn (or third round for 3-ply), following the colors in the stitch graph in your pattern, as shown. Do try to maintain your Fair Isle pattern on your sleeves, but don't worry if you notice slight irregularities or miscalculations. These will not be noticeable in your finished sweater; no one will see the underarms except you.

Continue in your Fair Isle pattern until your sleeve measures 8½" to 10" (or even 11" for a large person) across the top when measured flat. The distance around the top of your sleeve will be twice this flat measurement, or a total of 17" to 20" (or 22" for a large person).

Tip

An easy way to increase one stitch is to lift the stitch below the one you are increasing onto the needle and knit it.

4. Because of the stitch increases, Fair Isle patterns do not meet evenly at the underarms of sleeves. You can keep track of rounds between your sleeve increases by using a row marker that is easy to make from yarn. Just tie a 14" length of yarn into 4 consecutive loops (or 3 for 3-ply work), as shown. Slip the top loop onto your right needle at the beginning of the first row above the ribbing and move the marker up 1 loop as you finish each round. When you reach the bottom loop, you will know that it is time to increase a stitch. An added benefit of this type of marker is that whenever you lay your knitting down and come back to it later, you can tell at a glance if you are working on an increase round. It also reminds you at the end of the round that you need an increase stitch there, too. Our row marker is useful for any knitting project that uses a circular needle. This simple invention has thrilled many knitters and is available at no cost!

Beginning and end of row

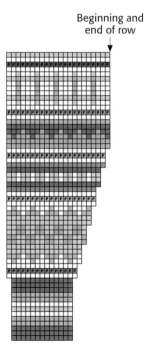

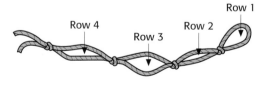
Row 4   Row 3   Row 2   Row 1

KNITTING THE BODY TUBE

Using the tubular method, cardigans are as easy to knit as pullovers, and, for many people, more practical to wear and more flattering. The body of a Philosopher's Fair Isle sweater is a large, straight tube, with just a few differences between pullovers and cardigans. Start by reading about the *steek* technique we use for both pullovers and cardigans, and you'll be ready to begin knitting the body of your sweater.

What Is a Steek?

For both pullovers and cardigans, we use a *steek* (a Celtic word meaning "closure") to indicate where to cut the knitted fabric apart. A steek is a single purl stitch made in every round. In a pullover, this purl stitch goes from the underarm to the top of the body tube on both sides. In a cardigan, there is an additional steek down the entire center front. After finishing the body tube, you will need to machine sew two lines of straight stitching as close as possible to these steeks so you can cut open the armholes to set in sleeves and pick up stitches for the button bands on a cardigan. Please be sure to sew underneath the steek for each armhole to prevent these stitches from running. See page 38, step 1. You will also need to machine sew a front neckline curve to stabilize your work so it is easy to pick up and knit stitches for the neckband.

Knitting the Ribbing

1. To start knitting a body tube, cast on the number of stitches called for in your pattern and knit the ribbing. Because ribbing is by nature elastic and stretchy, check your work after several rows to make sure it looks crisp and firm rather than loose or sloppy. After you finish the ribbing, knit 1 round in your background color, making the increases if necessary, before you begin to knit your Fair Isle pattern.

Tip

Knit one round in a single color before binding off the stitches at the top of a sleeve. This creates a single layer of knitted fabric, which makes it easier to set a sleeve into the armhole of the sweater body neatly.

5. After you finish both sleeves and before you start knitting the tube for the sweater body, check your tension again. Place a tape measure under a round of your knitting, anywhere above the ribbing. Count the number of stitches in 4" of your knitting. Repeat this process 4 more times, each time measuring a different place on your sleeve. Add these 5 numbers together to find the total number of stitches in 20" of your own knitting (don't forget to include decimals). Divide this number by 20 to determine your own number of stitches per inch. Multiply the number of stitches you knit per inch by the chest measurement you want in your finished sweater to determine the total number of stitches you will need for the body tube. Then choose the closest pattern size for the number of stitches you should be increasing to after the body ribbing.

Tip

After you finish knitting the sleeves, one third of your sweater is finished.

6. The tension we have used for our 2-ply patterns is 21 stitches to 4". We have found that for most people, this produces a comfortable fabric. However, many people knit a completely satisfactory Fair Isle at 18 stitches to 4". To use the patterns in this book, such people will have to make adjustments. Those extra 3 stitches over 4" that we use in our patterns will convert a 48" body size to 54" if your tension is 18 stitches to 4". Following step 5 above will give you the correct-size sweater.

Tip

If you are much wider in the hips than the chest, you can start knitting the body tube with a larger size needle than you used for the sleeves, decreasing the needle size gradually in the upper part of the body tube. You can also consider blocking your finished sweater to an A-line shape.

Tip

After 2" of Fair Isle work, you should check to make sure that the body is the right size. Some knitters produce a looser or tighter tension on a longer circular needle, and there is no predicting which. It is worth checking that this is not a factor for you.

Knitting a Pullover Body

For a pullover, continue knitting the body tube above the ribbing, following the stitch graph, until you reach the length where you want the armhole to begin.

Knitting a Cardigan Body

1. It is essential that your sweater be symmetrical. Check the stitch graph in your pattern to make sure that the middle stitch of your sweater front lies either at the center of your

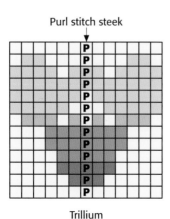

Trillium

Fair Isle pattern or between 2 motifs. To establish your Fair Isle pattern, place a yarn marker at the beginning of your first round to mark the first side seam. Divide the total number of body stitches by 4 to determine which stitch will be at the center front of your sweater. Following your stitch graph, knit to the center of your sweater front. If the stitch graph for your sweater has an odd number of stitches, as in the "Trillium" pattern, you can use the center stitch as the purl-stitch steek.

2. If your stitch graph has an even number of stitches, as in the "Windows" pattern, you will need to cast on an extra stitch at the center of your sweater front for the steek.

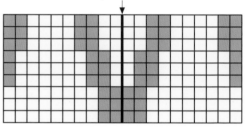

Cast on 1 *extra* purl stitch here for steek.

Windows

3. Place a brightly colored yarn marker before the steek at the center front of your sweater to remind you to purl that stitch. Continue knitting to the right side of your sweater, following your stitch graph, and place a yarn marker to mark the stitch at the right side seam.

Tip

Use both strands of yarn to purl the steek stitch. That way, it will be easy to see on the inside of your work and easier to cut when you are assembling your sweater.

4. When you have finished the first round of your Fair Isle pattern, take time to count your stitches again and make sure that you have established your Fair Isle pattern correctly. Continue knitting the body tube to 5" above the ribbing and add the pockets.

Tip

If you somehow miscalculate the symmetry of your Fair Isle pattern, you can move your side seam or row marker as much as 2" toward the back of your sweater. Much more distance than that will make the unevenness at the side seam look too prominent.

Adding Pockets

Our pockets are designed to rest on the ribbing, which keeps them from sagging or distorting a finished cardigan. With ribbing that matches the color of the background, they are virtually invisible.

1. For 2-ply Philosopher's Wool yarn, knit 2 pocket squares in your background color, each 29 stitches wide by 5" long. For our 3-ply yarn, knit the pockets 23 stitches wide by 5" long. Leave both squares on the needle.

2. When the body of your cardigan measures 5" above the ribbing, find the center 29 (or 23) stitches of each sweater front. As you come to them, put these stitches onto a strand of yarn and knit across the pocket stitches instead.

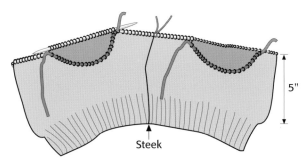

Steek

5"

3. To finish the pockets, see page 40.

Knitting the Armholes

The only other interruptions to the body tube of either a pullover or cardigan are the steeks for the armholes.

1. To calculate where you should start knitting the purl-stitch steeks for the armholes, add ½" to your finished armhole depth measurement. This will provide enough ease to make it easy to set the sleeves into the armholes when you assemble your sweater.

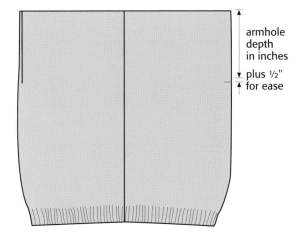

armhole depth in inches

plus ½" for ease

2. Place a yarn marker before each armhole steek and continue knitting to the desired finished length for your sweater. Knit the last round of the body tube in a single color, so that you can finish the shoulder seams and neckline neatly.

ASSEMBLING & FINISHING

When you have finished knitting the sleeve and body tubes, assembling and finishing your sweater could not be easier. All you need is a sewing machine, a sharp pair of scissors, and a couple of tapestry needles. After you try our simple techniques, you may never want to put a sweater together any other way.

For Pullovers and Cardigans

Using a pair of scissors to cut knitted fabric may seem frightening at first, but it opens up a whole new world of possibilities! To stabilize the steeks in a body tube, any sewing machine that can do straight stitching will work well. Thread the machine with a thread that blends with the colors in your sweater.

Tip

Give yourself a practice piece—machine stitch on a small swatch of your own knitting before you sew a steek on an actual sweater body. If the feed dogs on your sewing machine catch the stitches on the wrong side of your swatch, place tissue paper under your sweater before you begin stitching a steek. Machine stitch slowly.

1. Working on the right side of your sweater, machine stitch a U-shaped line of fine, straight stitching around each of the armhole steeks. Do a second line of stitching to reinforce the first. Use a fairly short stitch length and make sure to catch the top stitch on either side of the steek. Machine stitch slowly.

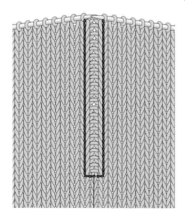

2. The front neckline takes up approximately one third of the stitches on the front of the body, and the shoulder seams each take a third of the front stitches. Using your Fair Isle pattern or the neckline curve of a favorite sweater as a guide, mark a symmetrical front neckline curve that is about 3" to 3½" deep on the center third of your sweater body. Machine sew the neckline with 1 row of stretch stitching, zigzag stitching, or 2 rows of fine, straight stitches. The neckband will not stretch, so make sure that the neckline of a pullover is large enough to fit loosely over the wearer's head. This can require a circumference of up to 25".

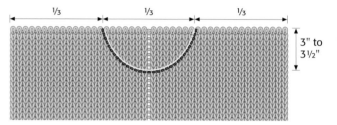

Tip

If you find that the neckline of a sweater is too small after you've already put it together, you can remove the neck ribbing, machine sew a deeper neckline, and knit a new neckband on the sweater.

3. Time to make the first cut! Remember that knitting does not want to unravel sideways, and that Scandinavians have used the steek technique for centuries. Using a pair of sharp scissors, cut the first armhole steek from top to bottom, taking care not to snip through your machine stitching. Repeat this step for the second armhole steek.

Tip

To overcome fears about using scissors to cut knitted fabric, make a small practice tube of knitting with a purl steek in it. Machine stitch on either side of this steek, just as you would for a sweater. Then cut your practice tube open—you'll enjoy the empowering feeling that comes from realizing that your knitting will not come apart.

4. Determine which shoulder will be the left shoulder in your finished sweater. Turn the body tube inside out and put the stitches for the left front and the left back onto 2 needles, making sure you have the same number of stitches on each needle. With a third needle, bind off the left shoulder stitches together. To do this, insert your right needle into the first stitch on both of the left needles at the same time and knit them together. When you have put the second stitch on your right needle, pass the first stitch over the second to bind off 1 stitch. Repeat this process until all shoulder stitches are bound off. This will create shoulder seams that are strong, not bulky, and beautifully neat. Bind off the stitches for the other shoulder in the same way.

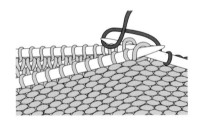

Tip

If you somehow have an extra stitch on one shoulder, simply knit three stitches together, instead of two, to fix your error.

5. To make sure that your sleeves and shoulder seams will form a nice, straight line after you set in the sleeves, lay each sleeve right side out beside the armhole of the sweater body. Check to make sure that the armholes on your sweater body are indeed large enough to accommodate your sleeves. Make sure that the underarms meet the lower edges of the sleeves and pin the top and bottom of each sleeve to the armholes with safety pins.

6. Starting at the bottom front of the armhole, set the sleeves into the armholes with a mattress stitch, as shown. Picking up the halves of the bound-off stitches that lie next to the sleeve, take enough of the sleeve edge in each stitch to keep it from puckering at the top; if necessary, take up extra stitches as you go and pick up bar stitches. For the armhole edge, use the closest clear row by the machine stitching. This stitch works beautifully and creates a very flat seam.

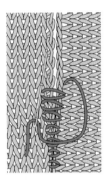

For Pullovers Only

1. Bind off the remaining stitches on the back neckline and, without breaking your strand of yarn, pick up stitches around the entire neckline, knitting the first round. Take care to pick up and knit each stitch just beyond (or on the body side of) your machine stitching and pick up the "bar" or "ladder" of each stitch, as shown. This will produce a crisp neckband with more definition.

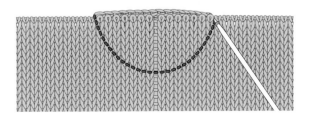

2. A finished adult neckband should contain about 90 to 110 stitches for 2-ply yarn and 70 to 80 stitches for 3-ply yarn. Check the number of stitches per inch in your sleeve and body ribbing, and multiply that number by the size you want your neckband to be. Knit your neck ribbing to match the ribbing on your sleeves and body. It should be approximately 1½" to 1¾" long.

3. Continuing in a single color, knit the neckband facing for the same number of rows. Bind off very loosely in ribbing and sew the facing in place inside the neckline. Use a loose hem stitch, making sure to attach each rib to itself so your neck ribbing will be vertical.

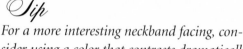

Tip

For a more interesting neckband facing, consider using a color that contrasts dramatically with your neckband ribbing.

4. Wait until after you finish your neckband to weave in the ends of yarn; then weave them in vertically. If you weave in yarn ends horizontally, as you change colors, your ribbing will tend to be distorted and lose elasticity.

For Cardigans Only

To assemble a Philosopher's Wool cardigan, follow the same steps as for a pullover, except for the neckband, pockets, and button bands.

1. To knit the neckband, pick up stitches starting at the center front, going around the back, and continuing to the center front again. Knit the first row as you pick up the stitches. Work back and forth in ribbing for approximately 1¾" and bind off the neckband in ribbing. Carefully cut away the extra piece of knitting above the front neckline from the original body tube.

2. To finish the pockets, put the pocket stitches from the yarn holder onto a needle and knit 2 or 3 rows of ribbing, working back and forth; use the same needle you used for the body of the sweater so the ribbing will not pull the pocket in. Use colors that match your Fair Isle work at that point so that the pocket ribbing is well camouflaged. Using a color of yarn to match your Fair Isle knitting beside the pocket ribbing, sew the edge of the ribbing to the front of the sweater with hem stitches.

3. With a size 13 tapestry needle, sew the lower edge of each pocket to the top of the ribbing on the inside of the sweater with hem stitches. The ribbing on the sweater body will stabilize the lower edge of the pocket. Sew the 2 side seams of each pocket with hem stitches, weaving in the ends of yarn after each seam.

4. We have developed a technique for making sure that the button bands on a Philosopher's cardigan will be neat and firm and maintain the pattern across the 2 halves of the front. Pick up and knit a bar stitch from every row of your Fair Isle pattern for each of the button bands, making sure to use a smaller needle than the needle you have used for your other ribbings. First, try 1 full needle size smaller and pick up and knit 24 stitches along one front edge. By doing this, you have knit 1 row. Continue ribbing for about 1½" more, using either a single color or changing colors as you plan to do for your button band. As you knit this small tension swatch, also make a test buttonhole by binding off 2 stitches in 1 row and casting on 2 stitches in the next row. Bind off in ribbing to finish your swatch. If the needle you used has worked well, your ribbing swatch will be firm, not puckery, and not so tight that

it pulls in. If your ribbing seems loose, change to a smaller needle and try again until your ribbing is firm and neat. Sometimes just binding off with a smaller needle will firm up the ribbing sufficiently. This button-band swatch is worth every minute it takes and can save hours of work.

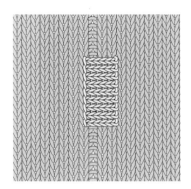

5. Take out the stitches in your swatch. For the buttonhole band, pick up and knit 1 stitch from every row on the body side of your machine stitching. Take time to determine where to place your buttonholes before knitting your button bands in order to space the buttons evenly. Remember that each buttonhole requires 2 stitches, or a total of 14 stitches for 7 buttons. Remember that you will need 1 less space between the buttonholes than the total number of buttonholes you make. For example, for 7 buttonholes, you will need a total of 6 spaces between them.

6. Count the total number of stitches you have picked up for the first row of your buttonhole band. You will need to reserve 3 stitches for above the first and at least 3 stitches for below the last buttonhole. Subtract 6 stitches (3 + 3) and the 14 stitches (7 x 2) used for the 7 buttonholes, i.e. 20 stitches (6 + 14), from your number of available stitches (X), divide that number by the number of spaces between 7 buttonholes (6), and you will know how many stitches you can use for the spaces between the buttonholes (Y). The formula works like this:

$$(X-20) \div 6 = Y$$

If there are "remainder" stitches, add about half of them to each of the 3 stitches reserved for the knitting above the top and below the bottom buttonhole.

7. When you knit the buttonhole band, knit the ribbing in colors that match your cuffs and waist ribbing and neckband, binding off the stitches for your buttonholes just before the halfway point and casting them on again in the next row to complete the buttonholes. When your ribbing is the correct length, bind off in ribbing for a flat finish.

8. Make your button band in the same way, omitting the buttonholes. At the top and bottom of your button band and your buttonhole band, knit (or crochet) a row in the color that matches the rest of your edging so that the same color will go all the way around the neck and waist.

Tip

For a woman's cardigan, buttonholes go on the right; for a man's sweater, they go on the left. For a sweater that will do double duty, knit buttonholes on both button bands. That way, you can place the buttons on one side or the other.

9. To sew the buttons on the button band, use a tapestry needle that will go through the holes in your buttons. Thread the needle with a strand of yarn, or use sewing thread if the yarn is too thick for the holes in your buttons. Hold a button in place on the button band and bring a threaded needle from the wrong to the right side of the button band, up through 1 hole in the button and down through the other. Repeat this process 2 or 3 times, winding the yarn once or twice around the yarn underneath the button for added strength. Bring the needle to the wrong side of the button band and finish off by weaving the yarn through your stitches and clipping the yarn close to the surface of the button band.

10. We could probably write a book about cutting—perhaps a psychological treatise or a discussion of timing. However long you leave a sweater lying around looking beautiful, at some point you will want to see it worn. When you are ready, take a sharp pair of scissors and cut through the purl stitch on the front of your cardigan. Tidy up any stray threads and there you are—your cardigan is completely finished and ready to put on!

CARING FOR WOOL SWEATERS

Philosopher's Wool yarn washes easily and feels much softer after the first washing. Our sweaters also grow 2" to 4" the first time you wash them. Because our wool has not been denatured by chemicals, acids, and bleaches, each fiber relaxes and elongates as the oils are washed out. This means that if your sweater is a bit on the snug side, you can easily make it fit more loosely by washing it. To wash a Philosopher's Fair Isle sweater, use a couple of squirts of liquid dish detergent and warm (to your hands) water in a large sink. Do not use Woolite or Zero; they will spoil the feel of Philosopher's wool. Allow your sweater to soak for a few minutes. Then swish it around in the water. Drain and refill the sink with equally warm water and rinse your sweater two or three times, until the water is more or less clear. The blackness or brown color you see in the water is from the spinning oils and lanolin. The lanolin in your sweater may be replaced with any one of the many products available on the market, or you can re-oil your sweater with a teaspoon of baby oil in the final rinse water. Put your rinsed sweater in the washing machine on a spin cycle; then lay it flat on a towel to dry in the sun or in another warm place. At this time, you can pat and pull the sweater to the size you want. If you are trying to enlarge a sweater considerably, use T-pins and a few thicknesses of towels and pin the sweater to the size you want. If you have lacquered wooden buttons, now is the time to rub a little oil onto each one to renew their luster.

CHANGES AND ALTERATIONS

Each year we work with forty wonderful ladies who knit Philosopher's sweaters for our store, both special orders and display models. Inevitably, mistakes happen: maybe a sweater is too long or the pockets were forgotten. We are all capable of making errors. We also receive phone calls from customers who need help with a pattern or a sweater that has not turned out the way they wanted it to. Any set of instructions can be misunderstood with the best intentions in the world, and we pride ourselves on working out solutions that involve a minimum of reworking or unraveling. The following ways to make changes, corrections, or alterations to remedy the situation may be helpful.

FIXING FAIR ISLE PATTERN MISTAKES

It is worthwhile to scan each round for any glaring errors as you complete it. Any mistake is easier to come to terms with sooner rather than later. If you follow these suggestions, it is extremely rare to need to unravel a larger portion of your work—unless it gives you satisfaction to do so!

• Unknit (take out) a few stitches, if necessary to correct a pattern.

• Mark the error with a safety pin. On the next round, drop the wrong colors one round, stitch by stitch, and pick them up in the right color from the yarn at the back.

• Mark the error and duplicate stitch it later, after your sweater is finished.

• If you have acquired an extra stitch, knit two together. If you are short by one stitch, make an extra one. No one will notice.

• You can also decide to live with the error—maybe it's the touch that proves the sweater is hand knitted and, perhaps, that you are not perfect!

CUTTING OPEN A PULLOVER

Ann's favorite cardigan started out as a pullover for Eugene. To change a sweater from a pullover to a cardigan, mark the center point and do two fine rows of machine straight stitching on either side of the center stitch or center two stitches. This uses up three or four columns of stitches. Then pick up and knit the bands on the body side of your machine stitching, cut the sweater open, and you will have a completed cardigan.

ADDING POCKETS

We call these retrofit pockets. Locate the position for the pockets—about 5" above the ribbing on the sweater front. If your Fair Isle pattern contains one-color rounds, pick up twenty-nine stitches for two-ply (or twenty-three stitches for three-ply) yarn on a suitable one-color round and do the same two rounds above it, leaving one round between the picked-up pocket stitches. If your Fair Isle pattern does not contain any single-color rounds, you can also pick up pocket stitches on any Fair Isle pattern round. Snip the middle stitch of the round between your picked-up stitches and take out the fourteen stitches for two-ply (eleven stitches for three-ply) yarn on either side of the snipped stitch. (Use these unraveled ends later to sew down the ribbing at the edges of the pocket.) Now you can knit the ribbing upward from the lower needle and the pocket downward from the upper needle.

LENGTHENING SLEEVES OR BODY

It is easy to lengthen a sweater, either by removing the ribbing and knitting until the body or sleeve is the length you desire and then re-knitting the ribbing, or simply by knitting a longer ribbing. To do this, snip one stitch in the row above the ribbing and unpick this entire round. You can now pick up the loops at the bottom of the body and lengthen the sweater as much as you wish. Bind off loosely in ribbing.

SHORTENING SLEEVES OR BODY

You need to decide how many inches you want to lose in the length. Perhaps some of this will be by shortening the ribbing. Calculate how much of the Fair Isle work you will eliminate, trying to be just above a band of pattern. Snip one stitch in the appropriate round and unpick the whole round. Put the stitches on a needle and re-rib to the desired length. Bind off in rib stitch.

MAKING A SWEATER LARGER

The easiest way to make a sweater larger is to wash and block it to the length and width you desire. You can easily make a loosely knitted sweater 10 percent larger in width or length. For tightly knitted garments, you may only be able to achieve a 5 percent increase in size, but on a 50" sweater, that equals 2½", which is often enough to create a perfect fit.

RUNNING OUT OF YARN

There are many reasons knitters run out of yarn. Everyone uses a different amount of yarn to knit the same number of stitches, some people weave in new colors for more stitches than others, and some cut off as much as 12" of yarn to weave in later. Because Fair Isle sweaters are multicolored, you can either substitute another color for the one you've run out of or simply purchase an extra skein. You may also decide to substitute another color lower in the sweater body and save the color you're low on for the area closer to your face. If the ribbing contains the color you need more of, you can remove the ribbing, take the yarn from there, and recreate the ribbing later with a different color yarn.

Coloring Sweaters with Philosopher's Colorways

Each of our Philosopher's colorways contains a palette of eight to thirteen colors. These colorways have become our trademark, and they are every bit as important as our patterns. In the photos on pages 46–61, you will see how beautiful and exciting each palette is, and how different the same sweater can look in a variety of colorways.

Our sweater collection is appealing because of the colors, the styles, and the "Philosophery" look. Part of this look is achieved with distinctive and multicolored ribbing. The nature of the coloring of our ribbing has varied over the years. We have used random stripes in different colors and of different widths; we have used plain bands with a pair of contrasting stripes; and more recently we have used single and double "color sandwiches." These sandwiches of color can be double at the wrist and waist and single at the neck and in the button bands. To make a double color sandwich, if M represents your background color and A, B, and C represent any three other colors, first cast on with M. Then, for two-ply yarn, knit three rows of M*, three rows of A, two rows of B, one row of C, two rows of B, three rows of A, and three rows of M*. For three-ply yarn, knit two rows of M*, two rows of A, one row of B, one row of C, one row of B, two rows of A, and two rows of M*. Repeat from * to * for a double color sandwich. You can use any symmetrical combination for a single or double color sandwich.

For some of the patterns in this book, such as "Stained Glass," "Tradition," "Garden Patch," "Southwest," and "Fractured Diamonds," you will find color prescriptions that indicate a specific number of colors and instructions for where to use each color. Other patterns, such as "Alligator Teeth," "Trillium," "Windows," and "Timber Frame," use two groups of contrasting colors randomly. In patterns like these, you will see red lines on the graphs. These lines suggest places to change colors so you can become accustomed to this random coloration process. For information on how to use dice to make color changes randomly, see page 20. After a while, your own artistry will take over and you will enjoy playing with the colors. It does not matter how many rounds of each color you use as long as you vary the number of rounds from color to color. Just take care to use each color evenly throughout your sweater to ensure good distribution and make sure you will have enough of each color to finish your entire sweater. Your balls of yarn should all get smaller at more or less the same rate. If you are not satisfied with the color progression in your sleeves, it is easy to change the order of colors in your body tube. Try shading in and out of color tones or use sharp contrasts between colors—both methods can work well in the same sweater. For example, in a sweater where the framework is done in one color ("Windows" or "Timber Frame"), change your background colors randomly, or shade them in and out, and add contrasting neck and button bands. Save your favorite shades for the top of your sweater, where they will frame your face!

Above all, our Fair Isle sweaters are rhythmic and fun to knit, and as you learn the patterns, your fingers will take over and do the thinking for you. As our simplified Fair Isle techniques and coloring methods become part of your repertoire of knitting skills, you will get an immense amount of enjoyment and pleasure from your needles and Philosopher's Wool yarn. Coloring your own Fair Isle sweater is a skill that gets easier and more exciting each time you knit a sweater. However you use your colors, if they are one of our colorways, we guarantee that your sweater will be both beautiful and unique.

THE COLORWAYS

FIRE

black, peat, dark brown heather, rust, wine, scarlet, MacRed, Anne
(Optional, not shown: barbecue red, barbecue purple, barbecue green, navy, jade)

NATURALS

black, peat, rust, dark brown heather, dark gray, medium gray, light gray, white

WOODLAND

white, navy, dark purple, grape, peat, dark brown heather, forest, light blue, light green, light purple, dark blue heather

(Optional, not shown: dark green heather)

COOL COLORS

black, navy, grape, Canadian strawberry, light Canadian strawberry, American strawberry, light American strawberry, orange, pineapple-orange (or lemon)

How to Dye Cool Colors

1. Nearly fill medium saucepan with cool water and ¼ cup white vinegar.
2. Add powdered, unsweetened soft-drink mix. Do not stir.
3. Put in 1 natural twisted skein. Start to heat on high.
4. After 1 minute, turn skein over.
5. After another minute, undo skein, leaving in dye bath. Push down with potato masher to spread dye throughout skein.
6. Bring to boil and simmer 5 minutes.
7. Turn off heat and allow to cool naturally or empty into sink and allow to cool naturally.
8. Rinse skein in warm water, spin in washing machine, and hang to dry.

Soft-Drink-Mix Flavors to Use

You can use these flavors in various concentrations to create different shades of the same color: Canadian strawberry, American strawberry, orange, pineapple-orange, grape.

FALL

black, dark brown heather, dark green heather, forest, scarlet, wine, peat, rust, Anne, cool orange

(Optional, not shown: barbecue green, dark gray)

PASTEL

white, light gray, dark gray, light blue heather, light green heather, light purple, dark blue heather, rose heather

(Optional, not shown: salmon)

NAVAJO

periwinkle, bright turquoise, turquoise, jade, rust, wine, scarlet, Anne, cool orange

(Optional, not shown: forest, grape, dark purple, barbecue green)

NIGHT SKY

black, navy, grape, dark purple, light purple, special dark maroon, special light maroon, dark raspberry, special raspberry, special rose

(Optional, not shown: dark blue heather)

BLACK AND BLUE

black, navy, dark purple, grape, jade, turquoise, periwinkle, light purple

(Optional, not shown: barbecue purple)

PEACOCK

navy, forest, dark purple, dark brown heather, peat, grape, light purple, dark blue heather, jade, turquoise

(Optional, not shown: barbecue purple, barbecue plum, barbecue green)

DEEP SEA

black, navy, grape, barbecue green, forest, dark green heather, Alberta green, jade, bright turquoise, turquoise, periwinkle

(Optional, not shown: dark purple, dark blue heather)

PHILOSOPHER'S YARN COLORS

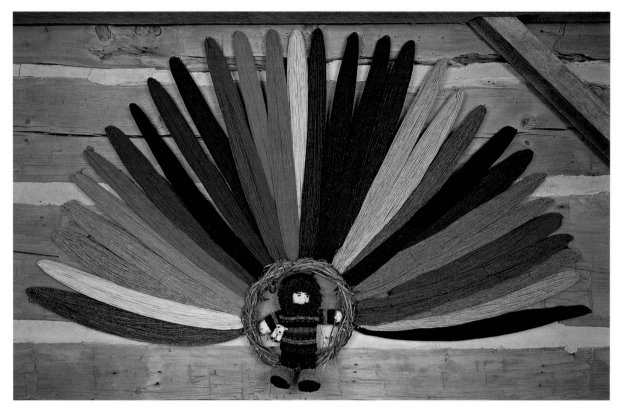

dark gray, white, medium gray, rose heather, salmon, light raspberry, dark raspberry, peat, wine, rust, scarlet, MacRed, Anne, yellow, dark brown heather, dark green heather, forest, Alberta green, light green, light blue, dark blue heather, navy, grape, periwinkle, turquoise, jade, dark purple, light purple, light gray, black

SPECIAL PINKS

rose, raspberry, dark maroon, light maroon

BARBECUE

barbecue green, barbecue red, barbecue plum, barbecue purple, barbecue yellow

THE SWEATERS

ABBREVIATIONS

K=Knit stitch
P=Purl stitch
S=Slipped stitch
St(s)=Stitch(es)

READING A GRAPH

*F*air Isle graphs are read from the bottom right-hand corner and from right to left, just as your knitting goes. Because there are only two colors in any round of your knitting, there are only two symbols (or colors) in any row of a graph. The only exceptions to this occur where certain graphs, such the one for "Rainbows," feature a P, to indicate a purl stitch, or S, to indicate a slipped stitch.

In the example below, the square with the **X** represents the yarn color you can hold in your right hand, and the square with no symbol represents the color you can hold in your left hand. Thus, a row that looks like this would start with three stitches knitted with your right hand, followed by one stitch knitted with your left hand. The pattern repeats to the end of the round.

As you work with each graph, the symbols or colors may change, either because you choose to make changes or because the graph tells you to make changes.

$\mathcal{S}$TAINED $\mathcal{G}$LASS

$\mathcal{P}$EOPLE OFTEN TELL us that our sweaters look like stained glass, and we agree. This "Stained Glass" sweater is a fine beginning Fair Isle project, because each tube starts out with one color, and the formula for the color progression is specified on the graph—all you have to do is follow the pattern.

Yarn:

3-ply chunky weight: 4 skeins black, 3 dark purple, 2 periwinkle, 2 turquoise

Needles:

For 3-ply yarn (see chart, page 27)

Tension:

16 sts = 4" in Fair Isle work. To make sure your sweater is the correct size, you must check your Fair Isle tension in the sleeve. If necessary, change needle sizes or pattern size.

Finished Chest Size:

39" (42", 45", 48")

Finished Length:

23" (24", 27", 29") or desired length

Sleeves:

Using the smaller needle, cast on 32 (34, 36, 36) sts in A. In K2, P2 ribbing, work 4 rounds of A, 3 rounds of D, 2 rounds of A, 3 rounds of D, and 5 of A. Change to the short, larger circular needle, and knit 1 round in color D, increasing evenly to 52 sts. Continue knitting, increasing 1 st at the beginning and 1 st at the end of every third round. Work 5 rounds in color A, 4 rounds in color C, and 3 rounds in color D, maintaining the increases as before. Now work from the graph, completing the sequence once, and repeat rounds 1 to 13 on the graph, increasing as before. You must change to a smaller needle for the following rounds or they will flare out. Knit 4 rounds in color A, 2 in D, 2 in A, 4 in B, 3 in D, 2 in C, 1 in B, and 1 in A, increasing, as before, until the sleeve measures 9" to 10" across the top and 18" to 20" around. Knit until the finished sleeve length is 19" (19", 19½", 21") or desired length. Bind off loosely.

Body:

Using the smaller size body needle, cast on 112 (124, 136, 148) sts in color A. In K2, P2 ribbing, work 4 rounds of color A, 3 of D, 2 of A, 3 of D, and 5 of A. Change to larger size needle and knit 1 round in D, increasing 44 sts evenly spaced across the round. 156 (168, 180, 192) sts are now on the needle. Continue working from the graph until the body measures 13½" (14½", 16½", 18½") long. At this point, follow the instructions on page 37. Continue following the graph until the body measures 20" (21", 24", 26"); then knit the remaining 3" in stripes of your remaining colors, using a smaller needle to avoid flaring.

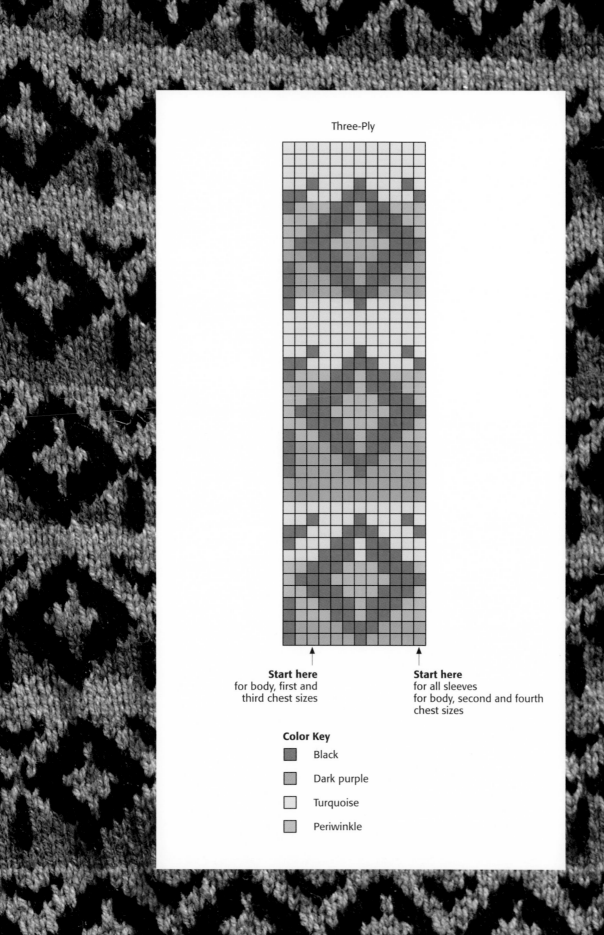

Three-Ply

Start here
for body, first and
third chest sizes

Start here
for all sleeves
for body, second and fourth
chest sizes

Color Key

Black

Dark purple

Turquoise

Periwinkle

TRADITION

THIS SWEATER IS as traditional as its name suggests. A broad diamond band frames it, and *peeries* (Celtic for "little bands") separate the larger diamond bands. Peeries are Ann's favorite element of Fair Isle design—not exactly surprising, since she collects miniatures. This pattern, with its classic design, has been one of our most popular.

Yarn:

2-ply worsted weight or 3-ply chunky weight [all 3-ply instructions are in brackets]:

For Eugene's version: 4 skeins navy, 2 forest, 3 dark blue heather, 2 dark purple

For Ann's version: 4 skeins black, 2 forest, 3 wine, 2 dark purple

Needles:

For 2- or 3-ply yarn (see charts, page 27)

Tension:

For 2-ply yarn, 21 sts=4" [for 3-ply yarn, 16 sts=4"] in Fair Isle work. To make sure your sweater is the correct size, you must check your Fair Isle tension in the sleeve. If necessary, change needle sizes or pattern size.

Finished Chest Size:

46" (50", 55") [39" (42", 45", 48")]

Finished Length:

28" (29", 30") [23", (24", 27", 29")] or desired length

Sleeves:

The ribbing should be multicolored. Cast on 52 (56, 60) [32 (34, 36, 36)] sts and work K1, P1 ribbing for about 3½". Change to the short, larger circular needle and knit 1 round in main color increasing evenly to 72 (72, 84) [48 (48, 48, 48)] sts. Continue following the graph and increase 2 sts every fourth [third] round, 1 st at the beginning, and 1 at the end, until the sleeve measures 9" to 10" across and 18" to 20" around. Continue knitting until the finished sleeve length is 19" (19½", 20") [19" (19", 19½", 21")] or desired length. Bind off loosely.

Body:

Cast on 176 (200, 224) [112 (124, 136, 148)] sts and work K1, P1 ribbing for about 3½" to match the cuffs. From your sleeve work, calculate so that you end your body with a full diamond. Change to larger needle and increase evenly to 240 (264, 288) [156 (168, 180, 192)] sts in the first round. Follow the graph until the body measures approximately 17½" (18½", 19½") [13½" (14½", 16½", 18½")]. Make sure the front is symmetrical. At this point, follow the instructions on page 37.

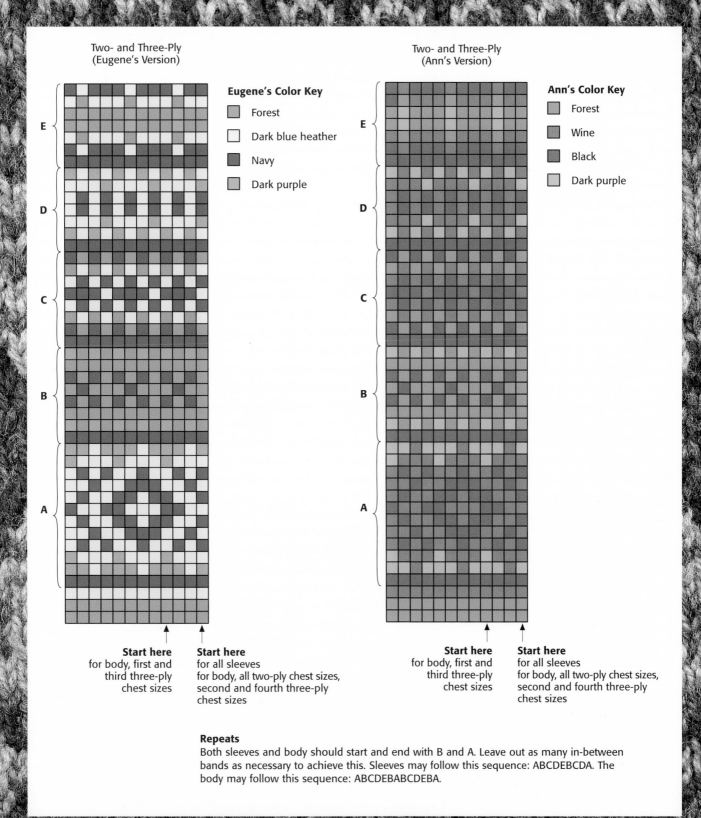

Two- and Three-Ply
(Eugene's Version)

Eugene's Color Key

- Forest
- Dark blue heather
- Navy
- Dark purple

E
D
C
B
A

Start here
for body, first and
third three-ply
chest sizes

Start here
for all sleeves
for body, all two-ply chest sizes,
second and fourth three-ply
chest sizes

Two- and Three-Ply
(Ann's Version)

Ann's Color Key

- Forest
- Wine
- Black
- Dark purple

E
D
C
B
A

Start here
for body, first and
third three-ply
chest sizes

Start here
for all sleeves
for body, all two-ply chest sizes,
second and fourth three-ply
chest sizes

Repeats
Both sleeves and body should start and end with B and A. Leave out as many in-between
bands as necessary to achieve this. Sleeves may follow this sequence: ABCDEBCDA. The
body may follow this sequence: ABCDEBABCDEBA.

Jenna Louise

WE DESIGNED OUR first children's sweater for our first grandchild's first birthday. You can knit this sweater in as few or as many colors as you like, and change the JLV design in band D to the initials you would like to use. We have found that children really love cardigans, especially with pockets. "Jenna Louise" is a perfect choice for a first "machine-stitch and cut" cardigan!

Yarn:

2-ply worsted weight: 3 skeins jade, 1 periwinkle, 1 turquoise, 1 navy, 1 dark purple, 1 Anne, 1 forest, 1 wine, 1 scarlet, 1 rust, 1 white (to be dyed orange cool color with soft-drink mix). Note that this quantity of wool will make 3 or more children's sweaters.

Needles:

For 2-ply yarn (see chart, page 27)

Tension:

21 sts=4" measured over stockinette stitch in Fair Isle work. To make sure your sweater is the correct size, you must check your Fair Isle tension in the sleeve. If necessary, change needle sizes or pattern size.

Finished Chest Size:

30" (34", 41") (ages 1–4, 5–9, 9–11 years)

Finished Length:

16½" (18", 21") or desired length

Sleeves:

Cast on 36 (36, 42) sts and work 2½" in K1, P1 ribbing in colored stripes. Knit 1 round, increasing evenly to 40 (44, 48) sts. Change to larger size needle. You will need 4 or 5 double-pointed needles until you have increased sufficient stitches to use a 16" (40 cm) circular needle. Following the graph, increase 1 st at the beginning and end of every third round, until your sleeve measures 5½" (6", 7½") across and 11" (12", 15") around. Continue knitting until the finished sleeve length is 11" (12½", 14") or desired length. Bind off loosely.

Body:

Cast on 140 (162, 200) sts and knit 2 to 2½" of K1, P1 ribbing to match your cuffs. Knit 1 round, increasing evenly to 156 (180, 216) sts. Change to larger size needle. Follow the graph and knit until sweater measures 10½" (11½", 13") long or desired length. At this point, follow the instructions on page 37.

Two-Ply

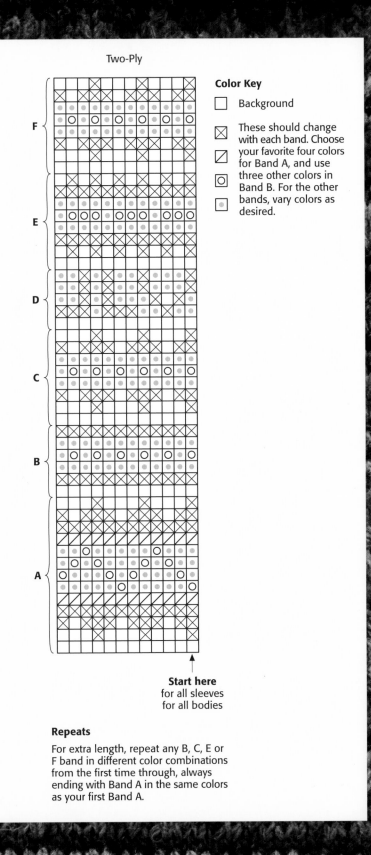

Color Key

☐ Background

⊠ ◪ ◉ ⊡ These should change with each band. Choose your favorite four colors for Band A, and use three other colors in Band B. For the other bands, vary colors as desired.

Start here
for all sleeves
for all bodies

Repeats

For extra length, repeat any B, C, E or F band in different color combinations from the first time through, always ending with Band A in the same colors as your first Band A.

COLOR YOUR OWN

FROM THE VERY first time knitters saw Jenna's first sweater, they asked for the graph to make themselves adult versions. This has become one of our most popular patterns. Most of this sweater's Fair Isle work comes in narrow bands (Celtic *peeries*) where the eight colors reappear in so many combinations that you get a jewel-like effect. It is the first of our designs in which you decide where to put the colors, and we guarantee that if you use one of our colorways, you will have a beautiful sweater no matter where you put the colors. Remember that your single balls of color should all decrease in size evenly as you knit. Choose your favorite four colors for the first band and the other three for the second band. Regroup any three colors for the third band, and again for the fourth, and so on. This design uses the weaving technique only in your dominant knitting hand (for most people, the right hand), and only ever uses one stitch from the other hand. This makes it easier to knit, so it is a good first two-handed project. There are also many one-color rounds to give you a rest from Fair Isle!

Yarn:

2-ply worsted weight or 3-ply chunky weight [all 3-ply instructions are in brackets]: 4 skeins black, 7 white, to be dyed with powdered, unsweetened soft-drink mix, as shown on page 51

Needles:

For 2- or 3-ply yarn (see charts, page 27)

Tension:

2-ply 21 sts=4" [3-ply 16 sts=4"] in Fair Isle work. To make sure your sweater is the correct size, you must check your Fair Isle tension in the sleeve. If necessary, change needle sizes or pattern size.

Finished Chest Size:

41" (46", 50", 55") [39" (42", 45", 48")]

Finished Length:

26" (27", 29", 30") [23" (24", 27", 29")] or desired length

Sleeves:

The ribbing should be multicolored. Cast on 48 (52, 56, 60) [32 (34, 36, 36)] sts, and work P1, K1 rib for 3" to 4". Change to the short, larger circular needle, and knit in rounds of graph pattern, increasing evenly in the first round to 60 (72, 72, 84) [48 (48, 48, 48)] sts. Increase 1 st at the start and 1 st at the end of every fourth round (every third round) until the sleeve measures 9" to 10" across and 18" to 20" around. Finished sleeve length is 18" (19", 19½", 20") [19" (19", 19½", 21")] or desired length. Bind off loosely.

Body:

Cast on 156 (176, 200, 224) [112 (124, 136, 148)] sts and work in P1, K1 ribbing for about 3½" to match your cuff ribbing. Change to larger needle and increase evenly to 216 (240, 264, 288) [156 (168, 180, 192)] sts in first round. Follow graph until body measures approximately 16½" (17½", 18½", 19½") [13½" (14½", 16½", 18½")] and you are at the beginning or end of a Fair Isle band. At this point, follow the instructions on page 37.

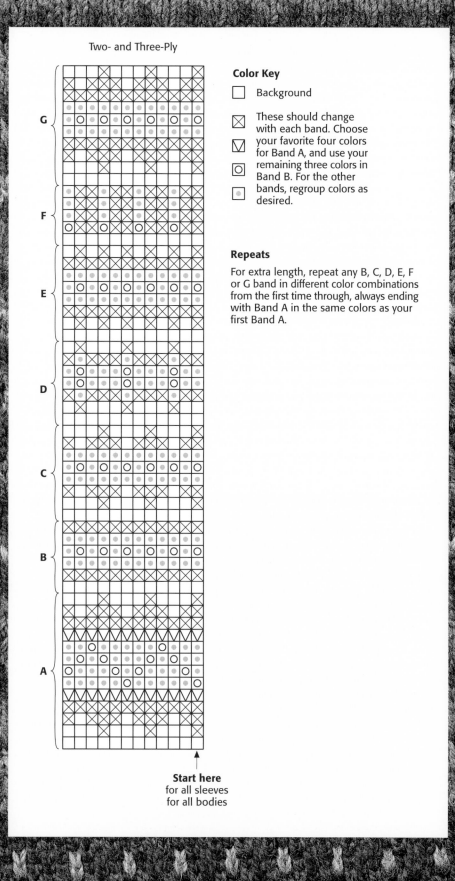

Two- and Three-Ply

Color Key

☐ Background

⊠ These should change
   with each band. Choose
   ◿ your favorite four colors
   for Band A, and use your
   ⊙ remaining three colors in
   Band B. For the other
   ⣿ bands, regroup colors as
   desired.

Repeats

For extra length, repeat any B, C, D, E, F
or G band in different color combinations
from the first time through, always ending
with Band A in the same colors as your
first Band A.

G

F

E

D

C

B

A

↑
Start here
for all sleeves
for all bodies

TRILLIUM

THIS SWEATER WAS designed for a competition calling for a picture of something inspired by Kaffe Fassett's work and having to do with Vancouver. Ann loves gardening and flowers. As a child, she started her first garden with just pansies—pansies of every color. This flower has a neat, three-petal outline, and since Ann's competition sweater was bound to be a Fair Isle design, she played with pansies. It is called "Stanley Park in the Dark" and is featured on the cover of the Philosopher's video. This sweater is composed of about thirty different colors and yarn from eight provinces. It didn't win in Vancouver, but the design was a huge success; when the motif is done upside-down, it produces trilliums—Ontario's provincial flower. In white flowers, the pattern can be made to look like clusters of three sheep in a pasture. Eugene wears this happily, symbolizing trilliums, sheep, and our neighbor Ontario Hydro's emblem all in one sweater. You can knit this pattern with one or more colors for the flowers and one or more colors for the background, and each round of flowers you knit will probably be unique.

Yarn:

2-ply worsted weight or 3-ply chunky weight [all 3-ply instructions are in brackets]: 1 skein black, 2 navy, 1 grape, 1 dark blue heather, 1 light purple, 1 special dark maroon, 1 special light maroon, 1 special raspberry, 1 special rose, 1 dark raspberry

Needles:

For 2- or 3-ply yarn (see charts, page 27)

Tension:

21 sts=4" [16 sts=4"] in Fair Isle work. To make sure your sweater is the correct size, you must check your Fair Isle tension in the sleeve. If necessary, change needle sizes or pattern size.

Finished Chest Size:

46" (50", 53") [40" (44", 48")]

Finished Length:

28" (29", 30") [23" (27", 29")] or desired length

Sleeves:

The ribbing should be multicolored, using stripes of several of your colors, or just the background colors. Cast on 52 (56, 60) [32 (36, 36)] sts and work K1, P1 ribbing for about 3½". Change to the short, larger circular needle, and knit 1 round in background color increasing evenly to 80 (80, 80) [48 (48, 48)] sts. Follow the graph, increasing 2 sts, 1 at the beginning and 1 at the end of every fourth [third] round, until the sleeve measures 9" to 10" across and 18" to 20" around. Finished sleeve length is 19 (19½", 20") [19 (19½", 21")] or desired length. Bind off loosely.

Body:

Cast on 176 (200, 224) [116 (132, 148)] sts and work K1, P1 ribbing for about 3½" to match cuffs. Change to larger needle and knit 1 round in background color, increasing evenly to 240 (260, 280) [160 (176, 192)] sts. Follow the graph until body measures approximately 17½" (18½", 19½") [13½" (16½", 18½")]. Make sure the pattern is centered before continuing. At this point, follow the instructions on page 37.

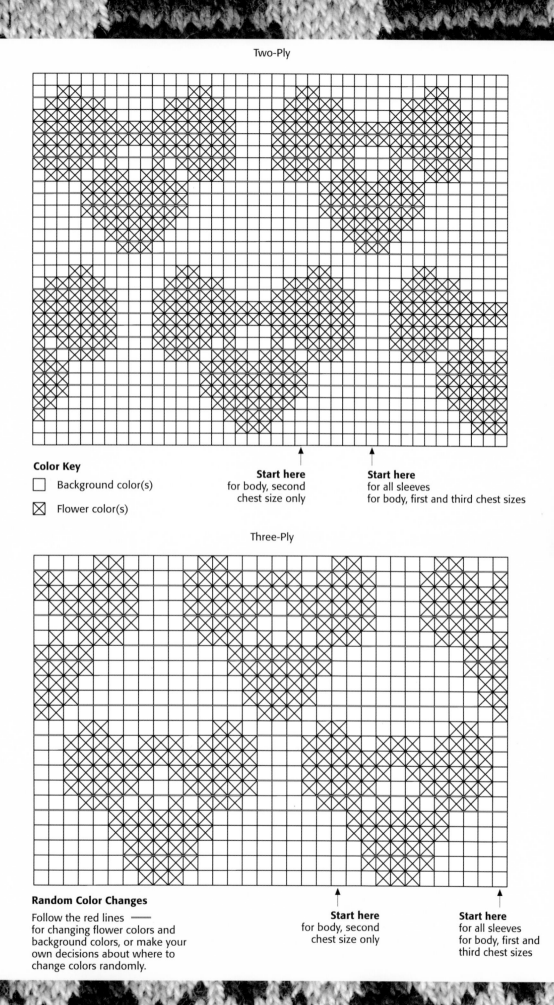

Two-Ply

Color Key

☐ Background color(s)

☒ Flower color(s)

Start here
for body, second
chest size only

Start here
for all sleeves
for body, first and third chest sizes

Three-Ply

Random Color Changes

Follow the red lines ——
for changing flower colors and
background colors, or make your
own decisions about where to
change colors randomly.

Start here
for body, second
chest size only

Start here
for all sleeves
for body, first and
third chest sizes

ALLIGATOR TEETH

ANN LOVES TO be able to knit without looking at a graph, and this pattern allows that and is delightful and rhythmic to knit. It is also the culmination of playing with giant zigzags that meet as pine trees and night sky. The final design works in a positive way to flatter the body, as your eye follows the vertical lines of the zigzags. "Alligator Teeth" was named for our son Alexander, also known as Uncle Alligator. You can knit "Alligator Teeth" in as few as two colors or as many as you like. We like the look of one zigzag progressing through color shadings and changing every three rounds or zigzags in one color with a randomly shaded background. Any ribbing style is perfectly suitable, but a corrugated ribbing looks striking, particularly in two-ply yarn.

Yarn:

2-ply worsted weight or 3-ply chunky weight [all 3-ply instructions are in brackets]: 6 skeins black, 2 wine, 2 scarlet, 1 MacRed

Needles:

For 2- or 3-ply yarn (see charts, page 27)

Tension:

21 sts=4" [16 sts=4"] in Fair Isle work. To make sure your sweater is the correct size, you must check your Fair Isle tension in the sleeve. If necessary, change needle sizes or pattern size.

Finished Chest Size:

46" (50", 53") [40" (42", 46", 50")]

Finished Length:

28" (29", 30") [23" (24", 27", 29")] or desired length

Ribbing:

This sweater can feature corrugated ribbing, which is a K2, P2, Fair Isle ribbing, with the purls all in the background color and the knits in different contrasting colors. Remember to take the purl yarn to the back of your work after each pair of purl stitches.

Sleeves:

Cast on 52 (56, 60) [32 (34, 36, 38)] sts and work K2, P2 ribbing for 2" to 3". Change to the short, larger circular needle, and knit 1 round in background color, increasing evenly to 70 (70, 80) [48 (48-48-48)] sts. Then follow the graph, increasing 2 sts, 1 at the beginning and 1 at the end of every fourth [third] round, until the sleeve measures 9" to 10" across and 18" to 20" around. Finish sleeve after the third multicolored zigzag: knit 2 rounds in background color for sleeves to set in easily. Bind off loosely.

Body:

Cast on 240 (260, 280) [160 (168, 184, 200)] sts and work ribbing as in cuffs. Change to larger needle and knit 1 round in background color. Follow the graph until body measures approximately 17½" (18½", 19½") [13½" (14½", 16½", 18½")]. Make sure the pattern is centered before continuing. At this point, follow the tubular instructions on page 37.

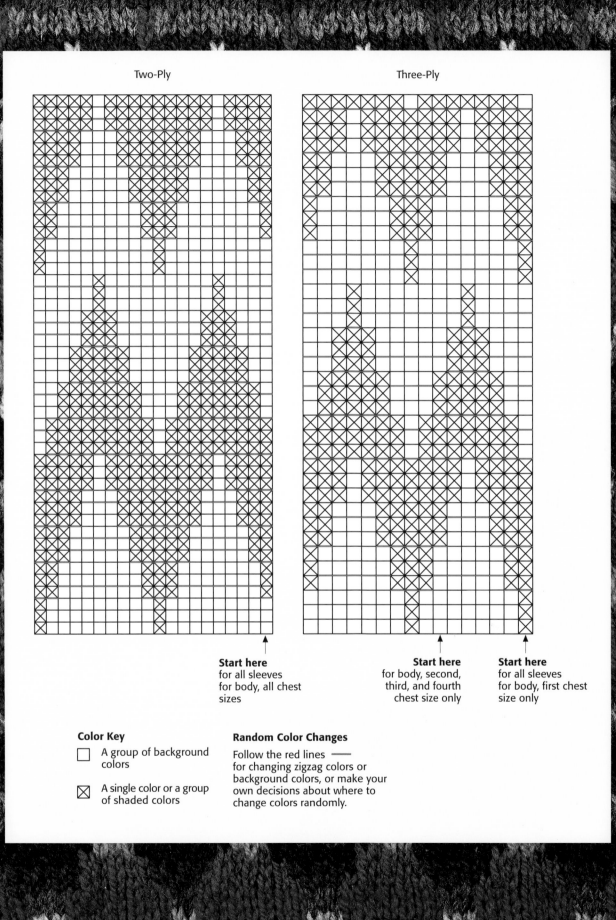

Two-Ply

Three-Ply

Start here
for all sleeves
for body, all chest
sizes

Start here
for body, second,
third, and fourth
chest size only

Start here
for all sleeves
for body, first chest
size only

Color Key

☐ A group of background
colors

☒ A single color or a group
of shaded colors

Random Color Changes

Follow the red lines ——
for changing zigzag colors or
background colors, or make your
own decisions about where to
change colors randomly.

TIMBER FRAME

*I*N 1979, EUGENE started to timber frame with Jack Spitzig. Jack was eighty and had built most of the old barns in our area. Eugene has timber framed six buildings since then, the largest being our warehouse, which is sixty feet by thirty feet and three stories high. Each time a new building is started, the oak timbers arrive and are laid out on our lawn. In fact, our lawn seems like a building yard during timber framing projects. The timbers have intrinsic beauty, and when seen from our bedrooms upstairs they form beautiful linear designs on the grass. This sweater honors both these shapes and Eugene's skill as a framer. The day we raised our warehouse, every "Timber Frame" sweater in the store was sold as a souvenir. This sweater also fulfilled Ann's desire to produce a vertical line sweater for knitting in the round, and it is perhaps our favorite design. In Fair Isle knitting, you should not change colors in vertical lines because this changes the texture of Fair Isle work. As you knit this pattern, be aware of this, and make sure that your tension is as you want it to be, or your sweater will be too small. Both graphs feature timbers that are three stitches wide, which produces quite different effects in two- and three-ply sweaters. Be careful to keep the color of your timbers in your left hand throughout to maintain even tension.

Yarn:

2-ply worsted weight or 3-ply chunky weight [all 3-ply instructions are in brackets]: 6 skeins black, 1 wine, 1 rust, 1 brown heather, 1 scarlet, 1 Anne

Needles:

For 2- or 3-ply yarn (see charts, page 27)

Tension:

21 sts=4" [16 sts=4"] in Fair Isle work. To make sure your sweater is the correct size, you must check your tension in the sleeve. If necessary, change needle sizes or pattern size. Because of the vertical lines to this Fair Isle work, you may need to use a larger needle than you would for any of our other patterns to achieve the tension you are used to.

Finished Chest Size:

46" (49", 55") [40" (44", 48")]

Finished Length:

28" (29", 30") [23" (27", 29")] or desired length

Sleeves:

The ribbing is designed to complement the sweater design: work ¾" in background color, ½" in a contrast stripe, ¾" in background color, ½" in contrast stripe, and ¾" in background color. Cast on 52 (56, 60) [32 (34, 36)] sts and work K1, P1 ribbing for about 3½". Change to the short, larger circular needle, and knit 1 round in background color, increasing evenly to 80 (80, 80) [48 (48, 48)] sts. Follow the graph, increasing 2 sts, 1 at the beginning and 1 at the end of every fourth [third] round, until the sleeve measures 9" to 10" across and 18" to 20" around. Finished sleeve length is 19" (19½", 20") [19" (19½", 21")] or desired length. Bind off loosely.

Body:

Cast on 176 (200, 240) [116 (132, 148)] sts and work K1, P1 ribbing for about 3½" to match cuffs. Change to larger needle and knit 1 round in background color, increasing evenly to 240 (256, 288) [160 (176, 192)] sts. Follow the graph until body measures approximately 17½" (18½", 19½") [13½" (16½", 18½")]. Make sure the pattern is centered before continuing. You may need to turn it a few stitches. At this point, follow the instructions on page 37.

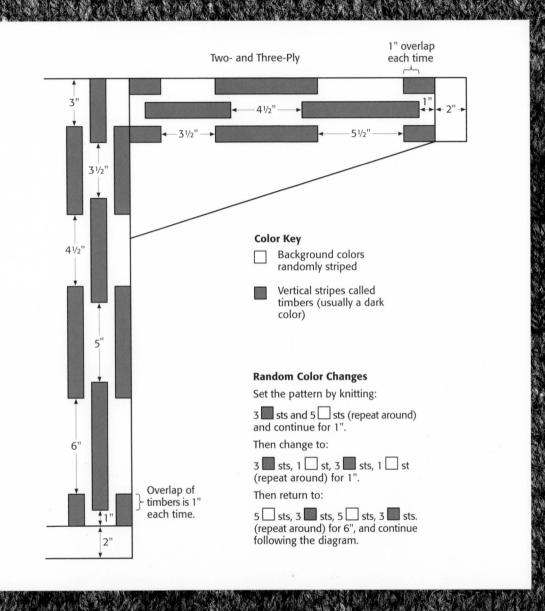

Two- and Three-Ply

1" overlap
each time

3"

3½"

4½"

5"

6"

3½"

4½"

5½"

1"

2"

1" overlap

Overlap of
timbers is 1"
each time.

1"

2"

Color Key

☐ Background colors
randomly striped

■ Vertical stripes called
timbers (usually a dark
color)

Random Color Changes

Set the pattern by knitting:

3 ■ sts and 5 ☐ sts (repeat around)
and continue for 1".

Then change to:

3 ■ sts, 1 ☐ st, 3 ■ sts, 1 ☐ st
(repeat around) for 1".

Then return to:

5 ☐ sts, 3 ■ sts, 5 ☐ sts, 3 ■ sts.
(repeat around) for 6", and continue
following the diagram.

Squares Around

THE PHILOSOPHER'S STONE in alchemical lore is concerned, among other things, with squaring the circle, and the name "Squares Around" is evocative of this. Our design features squares that are nine stitches by nine rows in three-ply Fair Isle work, with just two colors to each round of squares. We like the size of these squares; for the two-ply version for adults, we increased the square size to twelve stitches by twelve rows to maintain the same look in both weights of yarn.

Yarn:

2-ply worsted weight or 3-ply chunky weight [all 3-ply instructions are in brackets]: 11 skeins white, to be dyed with powdered, unsweetened soft-drink mix, as shown on page 51

Needles:

For 2- or 3-ply yarn (see charts, page 27)

Tension:

21 sts=4" [16 sts=4"] in Fair Isle work. To make sure your sweater is the correct size, you must check your tension in the sleeve. If necessary, change needle sizes or pattern size.

Finished Chest Size:

46" (50", 55") [40" (45", 49")]

Finished Length:

28" (29", 30") [23" (27", 29")] or desired length

Sleeves:

The ribbing should be multicolored, using a symmetrical effect to keep in style with the geometric nature of this design. Cast on 52 (56, 60) [32 (36, 38)] sts and work K1, P1 ribbing for about 3½". Change to the short, larger circular needle, and knit 1 round in background color, increasing evenly to 84 (84, 84) [45 (45, 45)] sts.

Follow the graph, increasing 2 sts, 1 at the beginning and 1 at the end of every fourth [third] round, until the sleeve measures 9" to 10" across and 18" to 20" around. Finished sleeve length is 19" (19½", 20") [19" (19½", 21")] or desired length, ending with a full square, if possible.

Body:

Cast on 176 (200, 224) [118 (136, 154)] sts and work K1, P1 ribbing for about 3½" to match cuffs. Change to larger needle and knit 1 round in background color, increasing evenly to 240 (264, 288) [162 (180, 198)] sts. Follow the graph until body measures approximately 17½" (18½", 19½") [13½" (16½", 18½")]. Make sure the pattern is centered before continuing. At this point, follow the instructions on page 37.

94

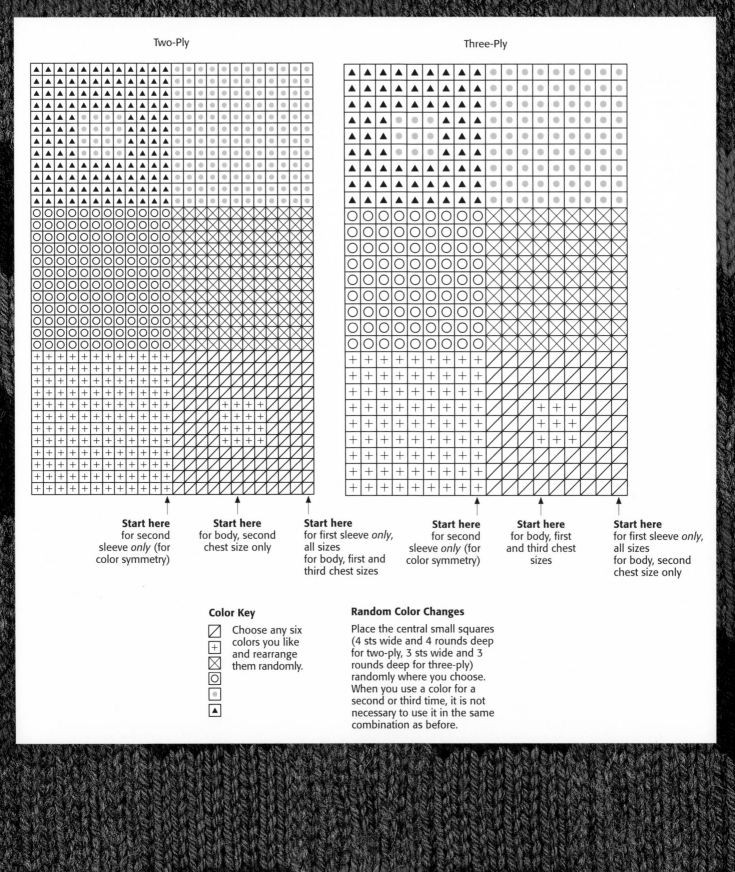

Two-Ply

Three-Ply

Start here
for second
sleeve *only* (for
color symmetry)

Start here
for body, second
chest size only

Start here
for first sleeve *only*,
all sizes
for body, first and
third chest sizes

Start here
for second
sleeve *only* (for
color symmetry)

Start here
for body, first
and third chest
sizes

Start here
for first sleeve *only*,
all sizes
for body, second
chest size only

Color Key

⟋	Choose any six colors you like and rearrange them randomly.
+	
⊠	
○	
●	
▲	

Random Color Changes

Place the central small squares
(4 sts wide and 4 rounds deep
for two-ply, 3 sts wide and 3
rounds deep for three-ply)
randomly where you choose.
When you use a color for a
second or third time, it is not
necessary to use it in the same
combination as before.

WINDOWS

$\mathcal{W}$E DESIGNED A sweater that was knitted in two halves from the cuff to the middle of the back, featuring an argyle-style design and Fair Isle techniques. This design produced vertical chains of diamonds. After this, Ann framed the diamonds with a lattice-like design that was also knitted sideways. Knitters who truly like the rhythm of knitting in the round asked us for the lattice design in tubular knitting, and this request became "Windows." Our farmhouse, store, and home all have over a hundred windows. We know this, because if Ann has insomnia and runs out of sheep to count, she counts windows.

Yarn:

2-ply worsted weight or 3-ply chunky weight [all 3-ply instructions are in brackets]: 5 skeins black, 1 forest, 1 dark green heather, 1 dark brown heather, 1 peat, 1 rust, 1 wine

Needles:

For 2- or 3-ply yarn (see charts, page 27)

Tension:

21 sts=4" [16 sts=4"] in Fair Isle work. To make sure your sweater is the correct size, you must check your tension in the sleeve. If necessary, change needle sizes or pattern size.

Finished Chest Size:

46" (50", 55") [42" (45", 48")]

Finished Length:

28" (29", 30") [24" (27", 29")] or desired length

Sleeves:

The ribbing should be multicolored, using stripes of several of your colors or just the background colors. Cast on 48 (52, 56) [34 (36, 36)] sts and work K1, P1 ribbing for about 3½". Change to the short, larger circular needle, and knit 1 round in background color, increasing evenly to 76 (76, 76) [52 (52, 52)] sts. Follow the graph, increasing 2 sts, 1 at the beginning and 1 at the end of every fourth [third] round, until the sleeve measures 9" to 10" across and 18" to 20" around. Finished sleeve length is 19" (19½", 20") [19" (19½", 21")] or desired length. Bind off loosely.

Body:

Cast on 176 (200, 224) [124 (136, 148)] sts and work K1, P1 ribbing for about 3½" to match cuffs. Change to larger needle and knit 1 round in background color, increasing evenly to 240 (264, 288) [168 (180, 192)] sts. Follow the graph until body measures approximately 17½" (18½", 19½") [14½" (16½", 18½")]. Make sure the pattern is centered before continuing. At this point, follow the instructions on page 37.

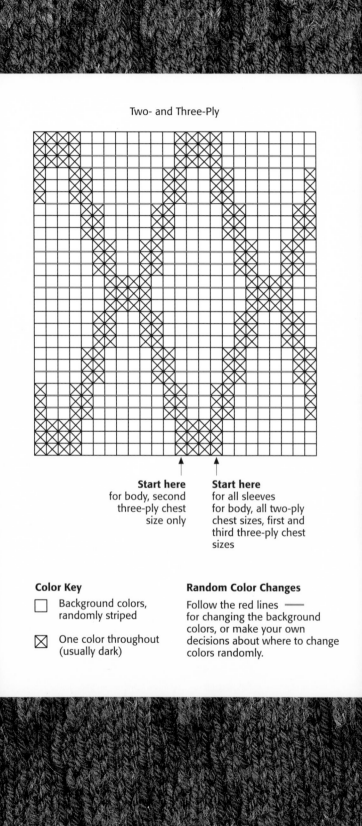

Two- and Three-Ply

Start here
for body, second
three-ply chest
size only

Start here
for all sleeves
for body, all two-ply
chest sizes, first and
third three-ply chest
sizes

Color Key

☐ Background colors,
randomly striped

☒ One color throughout
(usually dark)

Random Color Changes

Follow the red lines ——
for changing the background
colors, or make your own
decisions about where to change
colors randomly.

STARS

ANN KNITTED THE first "Stars" sweater like a painting, putting the different-size stars wherever she felt like putting them. She created a Milky Way effect diagonally across the front and the back. Each time she came to a point of a star, it was hard to tell which size it should be, so our daughter Cati VanVeen designed a regular graphic, so each sweater looks like a similar patch of the sky. "Stars" is an extremely striking design, particularly in "cool" colors, like a night sky of black and navy shot with lights of purple and jade. Since Ann likes sweater colors to be plausible, it has only been tried in nighttime and daytime sky colors, with various colorings of stars (and a little poetic license).

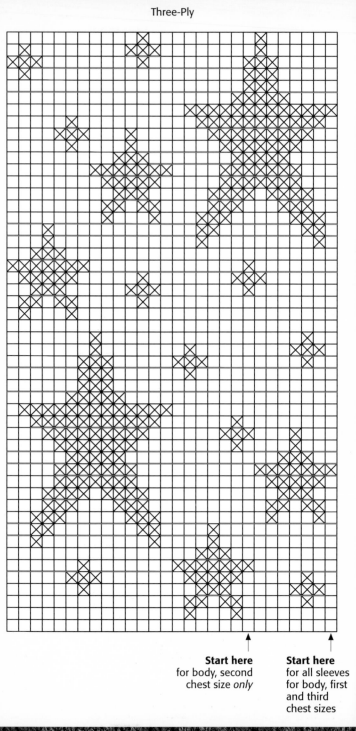

Three-Ply

Start here
for body, second
chest size *only*

Start here
for all sleeves
for body, first
and third
chest sizes

Yarn:

2-ply worsted weight or 3-ply chunky weight [all 3-ply instructions are in brackets]: 1 skein navy, 1 dark purple, 1 jade, 1 turquoise, 1 bright turquoise, 1 grape, 1 wine, 1 scarlet, 1 MacRed, 1 Anne, 1 cool orange

Needles:

For 2- or 3-ply yarn (see charts, page 27)

Tension:

21 sts=4" [16 sts=4"] in Fair Isle work. To make sure your sweater is the correct size, you must check your tension in the sleeve. If necessary, change needle sizes or pattern size.

Finished Chest Size:

40" (48", 56") [42" (49", 56")]

Finished Length:

27" (29", 30") [24" (29", 30")] or desired length

Sleeves:

The ribbing should be multicolored, using stripes of several of your colors or just the background colors. Cast on 52 (56, 60) [34 (38, 38)] sts and work K1, P1 ribbing for about 3½". Change to the short, larger circular needle and knit 1 round in background color, increasing evenly to 84 (84, 84) [56 (56, 56)] sts. Follow the graph, increasing 2 sts, 1 at the beginning and 1 at the end of every fourth [third] round, until the sleeve measures 9" to 10" across and 18" to 20" around. Finished sleeve length is 19" (19½", 20") [19" (21", 21")] or desired length. Bind off loosely.

Body:

Cast on 170 (202, 244) [132 (148, 188)] sts and work K1, P1 ribbing for about 3½" to match cuffs. Change to larger needle and knit 1 round in background color, increasing evenly to 210 (252, 294) [168 (196, 224)] sts. Follow the graph until body measures approximately 17½" (18½", 19½") [14½" (18½", 19½")]. Make sure the pattern is centered before continuing. At this point, particularly for the irregular stars, follow the instructions on page 37.

Two-Ply

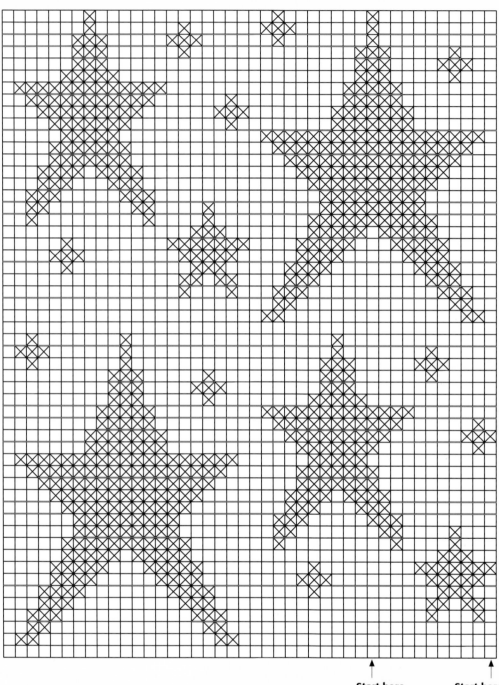

Color Key

☐ Background color(s)

☒ Star color(s)

Random Color Changes

Follow the red lines ——
for changing star colors and
background colors, or make your
own decisions about where to
change colors randomly.

Start here
for body, first
and third
chest sizes

Start here
for all sleeves,
for body, second
chest size only

SOUTHWEST

THE STAR MOTIF from Native American art seems to have universal appeal. Often it is used in a large and striking way that is totally unsuitable for Fair Isle knitting. In New Mexico, Ann saw the Native American star combined with the traditional cross on wallpaper in a rest room. It struck the perfect chord. This design is colored symmetrically to emphasize the motif's own symmetry, and we have color-coded these color changes for you to follow if you like. We have also suggested how many rounds of triangles, crosses, and stars to use.

104

Yarn:

2-ply worsted weight or 3-ply chunky weight [all 3-ply instructions are in brackets]: 1 skein wine, 1 white (to be dyed cool color orange with soft-drink mix), 1 Anne, 1 rust, 1 black, 1 peat, 1 dark brown heather, 1 dark green heather, 1 barbecue green, 1 forest

Needles:

For 2- or 3-ply yarn (see charts, page 27)

Tension:

21 sts=4" [16 sts=4"] in Fair Isle work. To make sure your sweater is the correct size, you must check your tension in the sleeve. If necessary, change needle sizes or pattern size.

Finished Chest Size:

42" (46", 50") [44" (49")]

Finished Length:

27" (29", 29") [27" (29")] or desired length

Sleeves:

The ribbing should be multicolored, using stripes of several of your colors or just the background colors. Cast on 52 (56, 60) [36 (38)] sts and work K1, P1 ribbing for about 3½". Change to the short, larger circular needle, and knit 1 round in background color, increasing evenly to 65 (65, 87) [54 (54)] sts. Follow the graph, increasing 2 sts, 1 at the beginning and 1 at the end of every fourth [third] round, until the sleeve measures 9" to 10" across and 18" to 20" around. (For the 2-ply sleeve, knit 3 rounds of triangles and 2 times through the main graph, followed by 3 rounds of triangles and random stripes. For the 3-ply sleeve, knit 3 rounds of triangles, followed by star, cross, star, 3 rounds of triangles, and random stripes). Finished sleeve length is 19" (19½", 19½") [19½" (21")] or desired length. Bind off loosely.

Body:

Cast on 170 (202, 244) [140 (160)] sts and work K1, P1 ribbing for about 3½" to match cuffs. Change to larger needle and knit 1 round in background color, increasing evenly to 220 (242, 264) [176 (198)] sts. For the 2-ply sweater, make 6 (7, 8) rounds of triangles. Then start with the crosses and 2 full repeats of the main graph, ending with triangle bands to the neck, then random stripes. For the 3-ply sweater, make 5 (6) rounds of triangles and 2 full repeats of the main graph, ending with triangle bands to the neck, then random stripes. Knit until body measures approximately 17½" (18½", 19½") [16½" (18½")]. Make sure the pattern is centered before continuing. At this point, follow the instructions on page 37.

Two- and Three-Ply (Graph for Star and Cross Motifs)

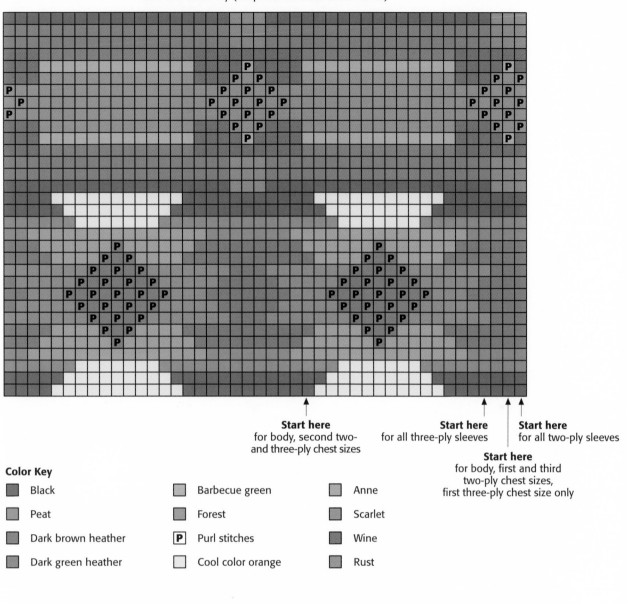

Start here
for body, second two-
and three-ply chest sizes

Start here
for all three-ply sleeves

Start here
for body, first and third
two-ply chest sizes,
first three-ply chest size only

Start here
for all two-ply sleeves

Color Key

⬛	Black
⬛	Peat
⬛	Dark brown heather
⬛	Dark green heather

⬛	Barbecue green
⬛	Forest
P	Purl stitches
⬜	Cool color orange

⬛	Anne
⬛	Scarlet
⬛	Wine
⬛	Rust

Two- and Three-Ply (Graph for Triangle Borders)

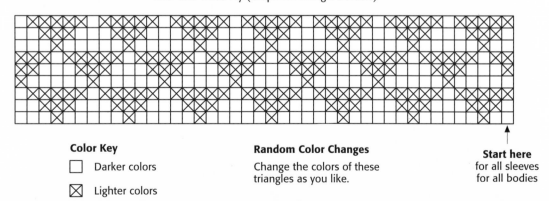

Color Key

☐	Darker colors
⊠	Lighter colors

Random Color Changes

Change the colors of these
triangles as you like.

Start here
for all sleeves
for all bodies

RAINBOWS

As SHE INSPIRED "Jenna Louise," our granddaughter, Jenna, inspired our second children's sweater, which was made to match her rainbow socks. You can knit this sweater in as few or as many colors as you care to use. We particularly like it in black, with six colors of the rainbow. We used slipped stitches for the first time in this pattern, which has really only a few Fair Isle rounds (in the diamond motifs).

Yarn:

3-ply chunky weight: 2 skeins black, 1 barbecue red, 1 Anne, 1 yellow, 1 jade, 1 dark purple, 1 barbecue green

Needles:

For 3-ply yarn (see chart, page 27)

Tension:

16 sts=4" in Fair Isle work throughout. To make sure your sweater is the correct size, you must check your tension in the sleeve. If necessary, change needle sizes or pattern size.

Finished Chest Size:

30" (36", 40") (ages 1–4, 5–8, 9–11 years)

Finished Length:

16½" (18", 20½") or desired length

Sleeves:

The ribbing should be multicolored, using rainbow stripes (black, red, Anne, yellow, green, jade, dark purple, black). Cast on 30 (32, 34) sts and work K1, P1 ribbing for about 2½". Change to the short, larger circular needle, and knit 1 round in background color, increasing evenly to 44 (46, 48) sts. You may need to use double-pointed needles at first. Follow the graph, increasing 2 sts, 1 at the beginning and 1 at the end of every third round, until the sleeve measures 5½" (6", 7") across and 11" (12", 14") around. Finished sleeve length is 11" (12½", 14") or desired length. Bind off loosely.

Body:

Cast on 120 (144, 160) sts and work K1, P1 ribbing for about 2" to 2½" to match cuffs. Change to larger needle and follow the graph until body measures 10½" (11½", 13"). Make sure the pattern is centered before continuing. At this point, follow the instructions on page 37.

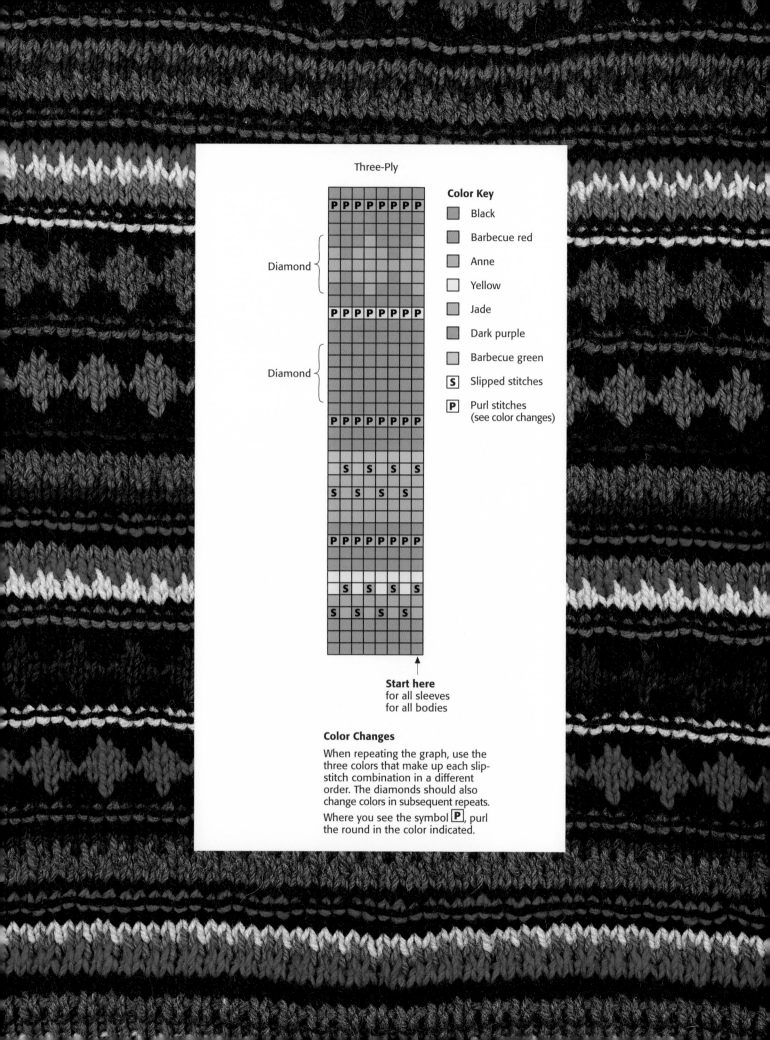

Three-Ply

Color Key

	Black
	Barbecue red
	Anne
	Yellow
	Jade
	Dark purple
	Barbecue green
S	Slipped stitches
P	Purl stitches (see color changes)

Diamond

Diamond

Start here
for all sleeves
for all bodies

Color Changes

When repeating the graph, use the three colors that make up each slip-stitch combination in a different order. The diamonds should also change colors in subsequent repeats.

Where you see the symbol P, purl the round in the color indicated.

GARDEN PATCH

GARDEN PATCH" is for customers who like the look of "Color Your Own" but want the colors to be specified. It is based, in part, on "Rainbows," which gave the purl ridges to this design. We have produced six combinations in six of our colorways, but customers have tried many other combinations. As with "Color Your Own," any good group of eight colors works well. If you come to a band with a specified color combination that you don't like, or for some reason you are short of a color, you can easily make any changes you want. Your colors will look pleasing whatever you do with them. The first "Garden Patch" sweater we did was in pastels, and the next in fall colors; both looked much like the rows in the garden, hence its name.

Yarn:

2-ply worsted weight or 3-ply chunky weight [all 3-ply instructions are in brackets]: 4 skeins white, 1 each of others in Pastel colorway

Needles:

For 2- or 3-ply yarn (see charts, page 27)

Tension:

21 sts=4" [16 sts=4"] in Fair Isle work. To make sure your sweater is the correct size, you must check your tension in the sleeve. If necessary, change needle sizes or pattern size.

Finished Chest Size:

46" (50", 55") [39" (42", 45", 48")]

Finished Length:

28" (29", 30") [23" (24", 27", 29")] or desired length

Sleeves:

The ribbing should be multicolored, using stripes of several of your colors or just the background colors. Cast on 52 (56, 60) [32 (34, 36, 36)] sts and work K1, P1 ribbing for about 3½". Change to the short, larger circular needle, and knit 1 round in background color, increasing evenly to 72 (72, 84) [48 (48, 48, 48)] sts. Follow the graph, increasing 2 sts, 1 at the beginning and 1 at the end of every fourth [third] round, until the sleeve measures 9" to 10" across and 18" to 20" around. Finished sleeve length is 19" (19½", 20") [19" (19", 19½", 21")] or desired length. Bind off loosely.

Body:

Cast on 176 (200, 224) [112 (124, 136, 148)] sts and work K1, P1 ribbing for about 3½" to match cuffs. Change to larger needle and knit 1 round in background color, increasing evenly to 240 (264, 288) [156 (168, 180,192)] sts. Follow the graph until body measures approximately 17½" (18½", 19½") [13½" (14½", 16½" 18½")]. Make sure the pattern is centered before continuing. At this point, follow the instructions on page 37.

Two- and Three-Ply

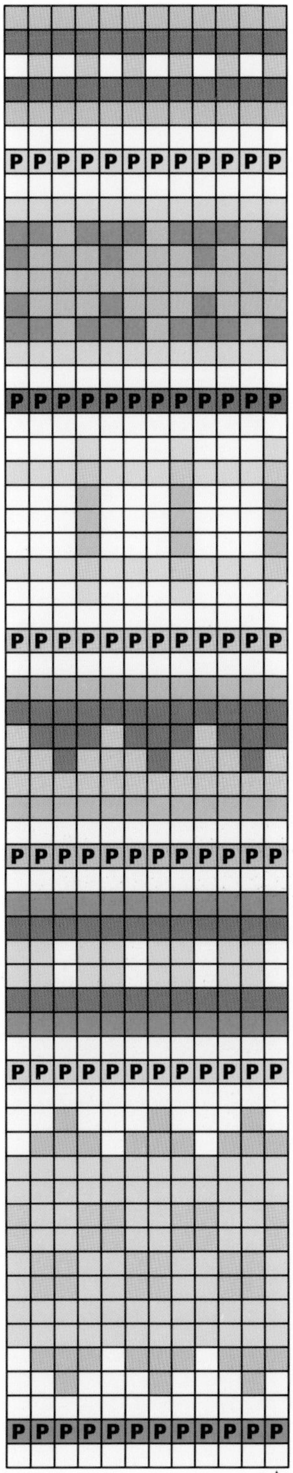

Color Key

- ☐ White
- ◼ Dark gray
- ▨ Rose heather
- ☐ Light green heather
- ☐ Light blue heather
- ☐ Light gray
- ◼ Dark blue heather
- ▨ Light purple
- **P** Purl stitches

Repeats

For extra length, repeat any of these bands using the same (or different) color combinations.

You may repeat these rows at the top of your sleeves and body if you wish.

Start here
for all sleeves
for all bodies

FRACTURED DIAMONDS

ANN HAS PLAYED with triangles and diamonds in many designs, and this combination of large and small triangles in just two colors is a pleasurable, simple, and classic pattern that can be worked in any two colors (or as many as you like). We gave it a corrugated ribbing to add extra interest, but any ribbing is suitable. For our customers, a regular ribbing gives the sweater a greater range of potential wearers.

Yarn:

2-ply worsted weight or 3-ply chunky weight [all 3-ply instructions are in brackets]: 6 skeins navy, 5 Alberta green

Needles:

For 2- or 3-ply yarn (see charts, page 27)

Tension:

21 sts=4" [16 sts=4"] in Fair Isle work. To make sure your sweater is the correct size, you must check your tension in the sleeve. If necessary, change needle sizes or pattern size.

Finished Chest Size:

46" (52", 55") [39" (42", 45", 48")]

Finished Length:

28" (29", 30") [23" (24", 27", 29")] or desired length

Ribbing:

This sweater can feature corrugated ribbing, which is K2, P2 Fair Isle ribbing with the purls all in the background color and the knits in different contrasting colors. Remember to take the purl yarn to the back of your work after each pair of purl stitches.

Sleeves:

Cast on 52 (56, 60) [32 (34, 36, 36)] sts and work K2, P2 ribbing for about 2" (this ribbing does not fold back). Change to the short, larger circular needle, and knit 1 round in background color increasing evenly to 75 (75, 75) [53 (53, 53, 53)] sts. Follow the graph, increasing 2 sts, 1 at the beginning and 1 at the end of every fourth [third] round, until the sleeve measures 9" to 10" across and 18" to 20" around. Finished sleeve length is 19" (19½", 20") [19" (19", 19½", 21")] or desired length. Bind off loosely.

Body:

Cast on 176 (212, 224) [112 (124, 136, 148)] sts and work K2, P2 ribbing for about 3½" to match cuffs. Change to larger needle and knit 1 round in background color, increasing evenly to 240 (272, 288) [156 (168, 180, 192)] sts. Follow the graph until body measures approximately 17½" (18½", 19½") [13½" (14½", 16½", 18½")]. Make sure the pattern is centered before continuing. At this point, follow the instructions on page 37.

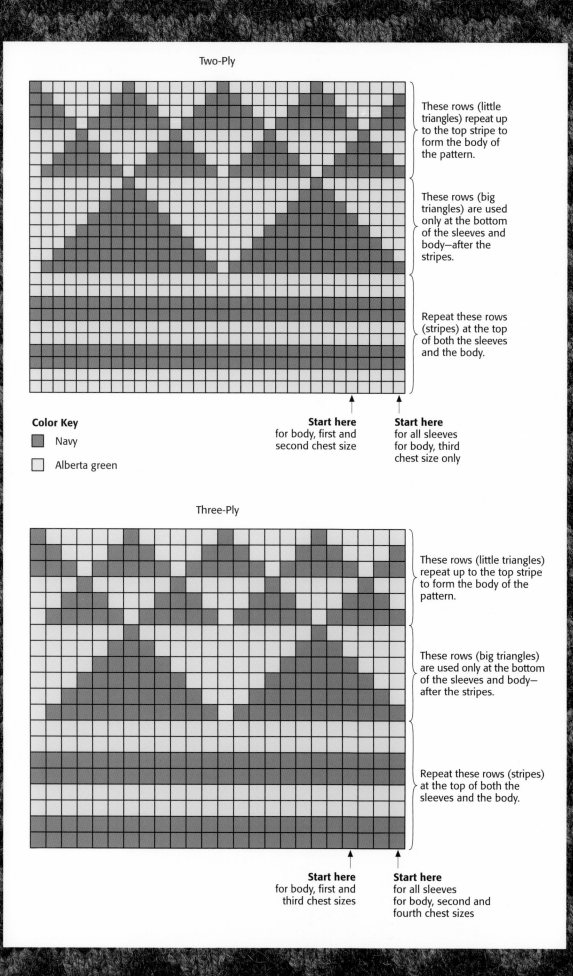

Two-Ply

These rows (little triangles) repeat up to the top stripe to form the body of the pattern.

These rows (big triangles) are used only at the bottom of the sleeves and body—after the stripes.

Repeat these rows (stripes) at the top of both the sleeves and the body.

Color Key

■ Navy

□ Alberta green

Start here
for body, first and second chest size

Start here
for all sleeves for body, third chest size only

Three-Ply

These rows (little triangles) repeat up to the top stripe to form the body of the pattern.

These rows (big triangles) are used only at the bottom of the sleeves and body—after the stripes.

Repeat these rows (stripes) at the top of both the sleeves and the body.

Start here
for body, first and third chest sizes

Start here
for all sleeves for body, second and fourth chest sizes

Fin & Feather Together

When Ann lived in England, her friends next door owned a collection of Escher prints that fascinated her. For many years, she wanted to try a Fair Isle design that incorporated this idea of positive and negative spaces, and "Fin & Feather Together" is the result. You can knit this sweater in any combination of contrasts, but the design is so complex that it does indeed seem to look best in black and neutrals or black and colors. Enjoy the challenge of this design: a contribution to environmental awareness. This sweater is definitely for experienced Fair Isle knitters because of the extreme irregularity and lateral movement of the graphic. For this garment, it will help to learn the pattern on the body and do the sleeves later, which assumes that you already know which size needle to use with Philosopher's Wool yarns and Fair Isle work. In the original sweater, halfway up the black birds become colored and the colored fish become black. The bottom round of fish is done omitting partial fish, and the top round of birds omits partial birds.

Yarn:

2-ply worsted weight or 3-ply chunky weight [all 3-ply instructions are in brackets]: 6 skeins black, 1 white, 1 light gray, 1 medium gray, 1 dark gray, 1 dark brown heather

Needles:

For 2- or 3-ply yarn (see charts, page 27)

Tension:

21 sts=4" [16 sts=4"] in Fair Isle work. To make sure your sweater is the correct size, you must check your tension partway up the body. If necessary, change needle size.

Note: Because of the complexity of this graph, it is given in a single size that fits most people.

Finished Chest Size:

50" [48"]

Finished Length:

30" [30"]

Sleeves:

Cast on 48 [36] sts, and knit ribbing as desired. After ribbing, increase to 72 [60] sts; then increase 1 st at the beginning and end of every fourth [third] round until you have 96 [72] sts and knit until you reach the desired length.

Body:

Cast on 240 [160] sts and knit ribbing as desired. After ribbing, increase to 264 [192] sts. Follow the graph until 18½" [18½"]. At this point, follow the instructions on page 37 for putting in the steeks. Bind off loosely.

122

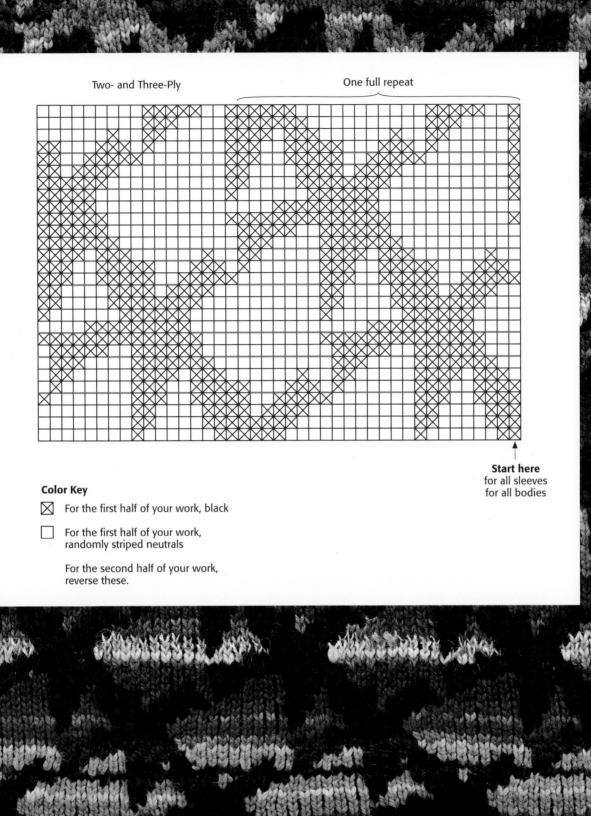

Two- and Three-Ply

One full repeat

Start here
for all sleeves
for all bodies

Color Key

⊠ For the first half of your work, black

☐ For the first half of your work,
randomly striped neutrals

For the second half of your work,
reverse these.

Kilim Jacket

$\mathcal{W}$E DESIGNED "Kilim Jacket" for our petite customers and for those who like a shorter jacket. It features a picot edge and stockinette stitch facing to the Fair Isle body. You can also use the graph with our regular style sweater and ordinary ribbing, following the instructions for "Tradition" (see page 70). The motif in this jacket comes from the traditional Middle Eastern Kilim carpets and wall hangings. It has been made using the tubular method. All the raw cut edges are covered by the facing. We've shown this jacket in the shorter version; a longer version looks fabulous, too.

Yarn:

2-ply worsted weight: 4 skeins black, 1 navy, 1 turquoise, 1 bright turquoise, 1 jade, 1 periwinkle, 1 barbecue green, 1 Alberta green, 1 dark green heather, 1 forest

Needles:

As specified in directions below

Tension:

21 sts=4" throughout in Fair Isle work: To make sure your sweater is the correct size, you must check your tension in the sleeve. If necessary, change needle sizes or pattern size. You will need a smaller needle to maintain this tension in the stockinette stitch facing.

Finished Chest Size:

39" (43", 48", 53")

Finished Length:

21" (22", 23", 25") or desired length

Sleeves:

Use a size 5 (3.75 mm) needle or whatever needle gives you 21 sts=4", either double-pointed or an 11" (27 cm) circular needle. Cast on 48 sts and knit 2½" in stockinette stitch. This will be your cuff facing, all done in the color of the crosses. Change to size 8 (5 mm) double-pointed or 11" (27 cm) circular needle. To make the picot edge, K1 *K2 tog, yarn over* repeat from * to * to end of round, K1. Next round, K into back of yarn over and K each stitch to end of round. Complete edging graph. Increase to 62 (62, 62, 62) sts in first round of pattern and knit sleeve tube, increasing every fourth round, until the sleeve measures 8½" (8½", 9", 9½") across and 17" (17", 18", 19") around. Continue without increases until the sleeve is ½" shorter than desired length (suggested length 19", 19", 20", 21") and end with rounds 1 to 4 of the edging graph. Bind off loosely.

Body:

Cast on 201 (225, 249, 273) sts with a size 5 (3.75 mm) needle and knit 2½" of stockinette stitch to make the facing at the waist. Remember to make a purl steek stitch at the middle of your work. This extra stitch is included in the number of stitches to cast on. Repeat the picot edge instructions and follow the edging graph. Change to a size 8 (5 mm), 32" (80 cm) circular needle, increasing evenly to 205 (229, 253, 277) sts, and continue with the body graph as in the sleeves. Follow the graph until the body measures 12½" (13½", 14", 14½"). Finish the tube with the first 4 rounds of the edging graph.

Front Bands:

The front bands are also Fair Isle work, following rows 1 to 9 of the edging graph. You will need to knit a test swatch, picking up 24 stitches, 1 for each round of knitting, to see what size needle you will use for your bands. For the Fair Isle band, use rows 1 to 9 of the cuff graph on each side, with a facing on the smaller needles. At the bottom of the bands and facing, leave a space to trim horizontally with rows 1 to 4 to match the waistband.

Neck:

Pick up about 92 sts. Knit 1 row in the color of the crosses. Decrease 6 sts in a second row and decrease 2 sts in the row before the picot edge. Finish the neck, using rows 1 to 4, a picot row, and the appropriate number of rows for the facing. Use 3 small clasps or 1 large clasp to close the jacket. An inside pocket (or 2) may be added if desired. For all other finishing, follow the instructions on page 37.

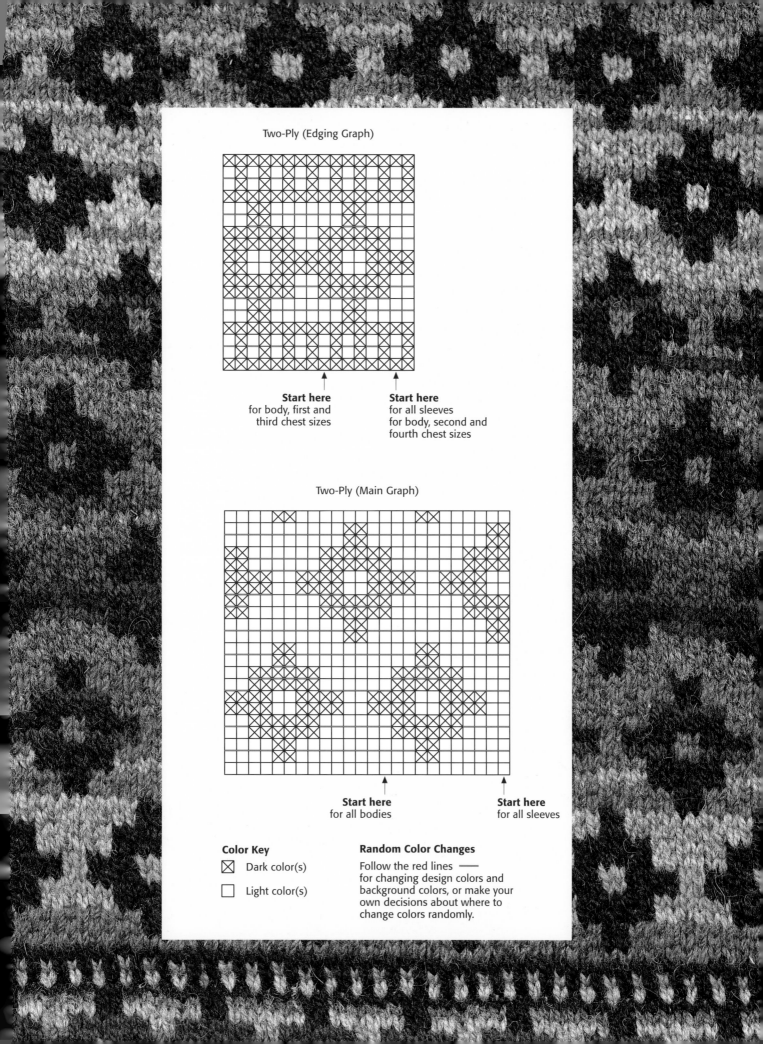

Two-Ply (Edging Graph)

Start here
for body, first and
third chest sizes

Start here
for all sleeves
for body, second and
fourth chest sizes

Two-Ply (Main Graph)

Start here
for all bodies

Start here
for all sleeves

Color Key

☒ Dark color(s)

☐ Light color(s)

Random Color Changes

Follow the red lines ——
for changing design colors and
background colors, or make your
own decisions about where to
change colors randomly.

RESOURCES

For your closest yarn store and information about ordering yarn, kits, and videos, please call or write to:

PHILOSOPHER'S WOOL
Inverhuron
Ontario
Canada
NOG 2TO
Telephone: (519) 368-5354
Web site: www.philosopherswool.com

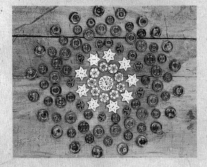
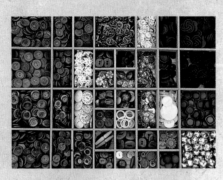

SELECTED BOOKS FROM MARTINGALE & COMPANY

CRAFTS

15 Beads: A Guide to Creating
   One-of-a-Kind Beads
300 Papermaking Recipes
The Art of Handmade Paper
   and Collage
Christmas Ribbonry
Creepy, Crafty Halloween
Gorgeous Paper Gifts
Grow Your Own Paper
A Passion for Ribbonry
Stamp with Style
Wedding Ribbonry

HOME DECORATING

The Art of Stenciling
Decorate with Quilts &
   Collections
Living with Little Quilts
Make Room for Quilts
Special-Occasion Table Runners
Stitch and Stencil
Welcome Home™: Debbie Mumm
Welcome Home™: Kaffe Fassett

KNITTING

Comforts of Home: Simple
   Knitted Projects
Knit It Your Way
Simply Beautiful Sweaters
Two Sticks and a String
The Ultimate Knitter's Guide

SURFACE DESIGN

Complex Cloth
Creative Marbling on Fabric
Dyes & Paints
Fabric Painting
Fantasy Fabrics
Hand-Dyed Fabric Made Easy
Machine Quilting with
   Decorative Threads
New Directions in Chenille
Thread Magic
Threadplay with Libby Lehman
Variations in Chenille

Our books are available through bookstores and your local quilt, fabric, craft-supply, or art-supply store. For more information, contact us for a free full-color catalog.

Martingale & Company	1-800-426-3126
PO Box 118	International: 1-425-483-3313
Bothell, WA 98041-0118	24-hour fax: 1-425-486-7596
	Web site: www.patchwork.com
	E-mail: info@martingale-pub.com